ANTI-INFLAMMATORY COOKBOOK 2022

QUICK RECIPES FOR BEGINNERS

LINA WHITE

Table of Contents

Lemon Buttery Shrimp Rice Servings: 3 17

    Ingredients: 17

    Directions: 17

Shrimp-lime Bake With Zucchini And Corn Servings: 4 19

    Ingredients: 19

    Directions: 20

Cauliflower Soup Servings: 10 21

    Ingredients: 21

    Directions: 21

Sweet Potato Black Bean Burgers Servings: 6 23

    Ingredients: 23

    Directions: 24

Coconut Mushroom Soup Servings: 3 26

    Ingredients: 26

    Directions: 26

Winter Style Fruit Salad Servings: 6 28

    Ingredients: 28

    Directions: 28

Honey-roasted Chicken Thighs With Carrots Servings: 4 30

    Ingredients: 30

    Directions: 30

Turkey Chili Servings: 8 32

    Ingredients: 32

Directions:	33
Lentil Soup With Spices Servings: 5	34
Ingredients:	34
Directions:	34
Garlicky Chicken And Vegetables Servings: 4	36
Ingredients:	36
Directions:	36
Smoked Salmon Salad Servings: 4	38
Ingredients:	38
Directions:	39
Bean Shawarma Salad Servings: 2	40
Ingredients:	40
Directions:	41
Pineapple Fried Rice Servings: 4	42
Ingredients:	42
Directions:	43
Lentil Soup Servings: 2	44
Ingredients:	44
Directions:	45
Delicious Tuna Salad Servings: 2	46
Ingredients:	46
Directions:	46
Aioli With Eggs Servings: 12	48
Ingredients:	48
Directions:	48
Spaghetti Pasta With Herbed Mushroom Sauce Ingredients:	49
Directions:	49

Brown Rice And Shitake Miso Soup With Scallions 52

Ingredients: 52

Barbecued Ocean Trout With Garlic And Parsley Dressing 54

Ingredients: 54

Directions: 54

Curried Cauliflower And Chickpea Wraps Ingredients: 56

Directions: 57

Buckwheat Noodle Soup Servings: 4 59

Ingredients: 59

Directions: 60

Easy Salmon Salad Servings: 1 61

Ingredients: 61

Directions: 61

Vegetable Soup Servings: 4 62

Ingredients: 62

Directions: 63

Lemony Garlic Shrimp Servings: 4 64

Ingredients: 64

Directions: 64

Blt Spring Rolls Ingredients: 65

Brisket With Blue Cheese Servings: 6 66

Ingredients: 66

Directions: 66

Cold Soba With Miso Dressing Ingredients: 68

Directions: 69

Baked Buffalo Cauliflower Chunks Servings: 2 70

Ingredients: 70

Directions:	70
Garlic Chicken Bake With Basil &tomatoes Servings: 4	72
Ingredients:	72
Directions:	73
Creamy Turmeric Cauliflower Soup Servings: 4	74
Ingredients:	74
Directions:	75
Mushroom, Kale, And Sweet Potato Brown Rice	76
Ingredients:	76
Baked Tilapia Recipe With Pecan Rosemary Topping	78
Ingredients:	78
Black Bean Tortilla Wrap Servings: 2	80
Ingredients:	80
Directions:	80
White Bean Chicken With Winter Green Vegetables	81
Ingredients:	81
Directions:	82
Herbed Baked Salmon Servings: 2	83
Ingredients:	83
Directions:	83
Greek Yogurt Chicken Salad	85
Ingredients:	85
Directions:	85
Pounded Chickpea Salad	86
Ingredients:	86
Directions:	87
Valencia Salad Servings: 10	88

Ingredients: 88

Directions: 89

"Eat Your Greens" Soup Servings: 4 90

Ingredients: 90

Directions: 91

Miso Salmon And Green Beans Servings: 4 92

Ingredients: 92

Directions: 92

Leek, Chicken, And Spinach Soup Servings: 4 93

Ingredients: 93

Directions: 93

Dark Choco Bombs Servings: 24 95

Ingredients: 95

Directions: 95

Italian Stuffed Peppers Servings: 6 96

Ingredients: 96

Directions: 96

Smoked Trout Wrapped In Lettuce Servings: 4 98

Ingredients: 98

Directions: 99

Devilled Egg Salad Ingredients: 100

Directions: 100

Sesame-tamari Baked Chicken With Green Beans 102

Ingredients: 102

Directions: 102

Ginger Chicken Stew Servings: 6 104

Ingredients: 104

Directions: 105

Creamy Garbano Salad Ingredients: 106

Directions: 107

Carrot Noodles With Ginger Lime Peanut Sauce 109

Ingredients: 109

Directions: 109

Roasted Vegetables With Sweet Potatoes And White Beans 111

Ingredients: 111

Directions: 112

Kale Salad Servings: 1 113

Ingredients: 113

Directions: 113

Coconut And Hazelnut Chilled Glass Servings: 1 115

Ingredients: 115

Directions: 115

Cool Garbanzo And Spinach Beans Servings: 4 116

Ingredients: 116

Directions: 116

Taro Leaves In Coconut Sauce Servings: 5 117

Ingredients: 117

Directions: 117

Roasted Tofu And Greens Servings: 4 118

Ingredients: 118

Directions: 118

Meatball Taco Bowls Ingredients: 120

Directions: 121

Avocado Pesto Zoodles With Salmon Servings: 4 123

Ingredients: 123

Directions: 123

Turmeric-spiced Sweet Potatoes, Apple, And Onion With Chicken 125

Ingredients: 125

Seared Herbed Salmon Steak Servings: 4 127

Ingredients: 127

Directions: 127

Tofu And Italian-seasoned Summer Vegetables Servings: 4 129

Ingredients: 129

Directions: 129

Strawberry And Goat Cheese Salad Ingredients: 131

Directions: 131

Turmeric Cauliflower And Cod Stew Servings: 4 133

Ingredients: 133

Directions: 133

Walnuts And Asparagus Delight Servings: 4 135

Ingredients: 135

Directions: 135

Alfredo Zucchini Pasta Ingredients: 136

Directions: 136

Quinoa Turkey Chicken Ingredients: 138

Directions: 139

Garlic & Squash Noodles Servings: 4 141

Ingredients: 141

Directions: 142

Steamed Trout With Red Bean And Chili Salsa Servings: 1 143

Ingredients: 143

Directions: 144

Sweet Potato And Turkey Soup Servings: 4 145

Ingredients: 145

Directions: 146

Miso Broiled Salmon Servings: 2 147

Ingredients: 147

Directions: 147

Simply Sautéed Flaky Fillet Servings: 6 149

Ingredients: 149

Directions: 149

Pork Carnitas Servings: 10 150

Ingredients: 150

Directions: 151

White Fish Chowder With Vegetables 152

Servings: 6 To 8 152

Ingredients: 152

Directions: 152

Lemony Mussels Servings: 4 154

Ingredients: 154

Directions: 154

Lime & Chili Salmon Servings: 2 155

Ingredients: 155

Directions: 155

Cheesy Tuna Pasta Servings: 3-4 156

Ingredients: 156

Directions: 156

Coconut Crusted Fish Strips Servings: 4 158

Ingredients: 158

Directions: 159

Mexican Fish Servings: 2 160

Ingredients: 160

Directions: 160

Trout With Cucumber Salsa Servings: 4 162

Ingredients: 162

Lemon Zoodles With Shrimp Servings: 4 164

Ingredients: 164

Directions: 164

Crispy Shrimp Servings: 4 166

Ingredients: 166

Directions: 166

Broiled Sea Bass Servings: 2 167

Ingredients: 167

Directions: 167

Salmon Cakes Servings: 4 168

Ingredients: 168

Directions: 168

Spicy Cod Servings: 4 169

Ingredients: 169

Directions: 169

Smoked Trout Spread Servings: 2 170

Ingredients: 170

Directions: 170

Tuna And Shallots Servings: 4 172

Ingredients: 172

Directions: 172

Lemon Pepper Shrimp Servings: 2 173

Ingredients: 173

Directions: 173

Hot Tuna Steak Servings: 6 174

Ingredients: 174

Directions: 174

Cajun Salmon Servings: 2 176

Ingredients: 176

Directions: 176

Quinoa Salmon Bowl With Vegetables 177

Servings: 4 177

Ingredients: 177

Crumbed Fish Servings: 4 179

Ingredients: 179

Directions: 179

Simple Salmon Patties Servings: 4 180

Ingredients: 180

Directions: 181

Popcorn Shrimp Servings: 4 182

Ingredients: 182

Directions: 183

Spicy Baked Fish Servings: 5 184

Ingredients: 184

Directions: 184

Paprika Tuna Servings: 4 185

Ingredients: 185

Directions: 185

Fish Patties Servings: 2 186

Ingredients: 186

Directions: 186

Seared Scallops With Honey Servings: 4 187

Ingredients: 187

Directions: 187

Cod Fillets With Shiitake Mushrooms Servings: 4 189

Ingredients: 189

Directions: 189

Broiled White Sea Bass Servings: 2 191

Ingredients: 191

Directions: 191

Baked Tomato Hake Servings: 4-5 192

Ingredients: 192

Directions: 192

Seared Haddock With Beets Servings: 4 194

Ingredients: 194

Heartfelt Tuna Melt Servings: 4 196

Ingredients: 196

Directions: 196

Lemon Salmon With Kaffir Lime Servings: 8 198

Ingredients: 198

Directions: 198

Tender Salmon In Mustard Sauce Servings: 2 200

Ingredients: 200

Directions: 200

Crab Salad Servings: 4 202
    Ingredients: 202
    Directions: 202
Baked Salmon With Miso Sauce Servings: 4 203
    Ingredients: 203
    Directions: 203
Herb-coated Baked Cod With Honey Servings: 2 205
    Ingredients: 205
    Directions: 205
Parmesan Cod Mix Servings: 4 207
    Ingredients: 207
    Directions: 207
Crispy Garlic Shrimp Servings: 4 208
    Ingredients: 208
    Directions: 208
Creamy Sea Bass Mix Servings: 4 209
    Ingredients: 209
    Directions: 209
Cucumber Ahi Poke Servings: 4 210
    Ingredients: 210
Minty Cod Mix Servings: 4 212
    Ingredients: 212
    Directions: 212
Lemony & Creamy Tilapia Servings: 4 214
    Ingredients: 214
    Directions: 214
Fish Tacos Servings: 4 216

Ingredients: 216

Directions: 217

Ginger Sea Bass Mix Servings: 4 218

Ingredients: 218

Directions: 218

Lemon Buttery Shrimp Rice Servings: 3

Cooking Time: 10 Minutes

Ingredients:

¼ cup cooked wild rice

½ tsp. Butter divided

¼ tsp. olive oil

1 cup raw shrimps, shelled, deveined, drained ¼ cup frozen peas, thawed, rinsed, drained

1 Tbsp. lemon juice, freshly squeezed

1 Tbsp. chives, minced

Pinch of sea salt, to taste

Directions:

1. Pour ¼ tsp. Butter and oil into wok set over medium heat. Add in shrimps and peas. Sauté until shrimps are coral pink, about 5 to 7 minutes.

2. Add in wild rice and cook until well heated—season with salt and butter.

3. Transfer to a plate. Sprinkle chives and lemon juice on top.

Serve.

Nutrition Info: Calories 510 Carbs: 0g Fat: 0g Protein: 0g

Shrimp-lime Bake With Zucchini And Corn

Servings: 4

Cooking Time: 20 Minutes

Ingredients:

1 tablespoon extra-virgin olive oil

2 small zucchinis, cut into ¼-inch dice

1 cup frozen corn kernels

2 scallions, thinly sliced

1 teaspoon salt

½ teaspoon ground cumin

½ teaspoon chipotle chili powder

1-pound peeled shrimp, thawed if necessary

1 tablespoon finely chopped fresh cilantro

Zest and juice of 1 lime

Directions:

1. Preheat the oven to 400°F. Grease the baking sheet with the oil.

2. On the baking sheet, combine the zucchini, corn, scallions, salt, cumin, and chile powder and mix well. Arrange in a single layer.

3. Add the shrimp on top. Roast within 15 to 20 minutes.

4. Put the cilantro and lime zest and juice, stir to combine, and serve.

Nutrition Info: Calories 184 Total Fat: 5g Total Carbohydrates: 11g Sugar: 3g Fiber: 2g Protein: 26g Sodium: 846mg

Cauliflower Soup Servings: 10

Cooking Time: 10 Minutes

Ingredients:

¾ cup of water

2 teaspoon of olive oil

1 onion, diced

1 head of cauliflower, only the florets

1 can of full-fat coconut milk

1 teaspoon of turmeric

1 teaspoon of ginger

1 teaspoon raw honey

Directions:

1. Put all of the fixings into a large stockpot, and boil for about 10 minutes.

2. Use an immersion blender to blend and make the soup smooth.

Serve.

Nutrition Info: Total Carbohydrates 7g Dietary Fiber: 2g Net Carbs: Protein: 2g Total Fat: 11g Calories: 129

Sweet Potato Black Bean Burgers *Servings: 6*

Cooking Time: 10 Minutes

Ingredients:

1/2 jalapeno, seeded and diced

1/2 cup quinoa

6 whole-grain hamburger buns

1 can black beans, rinsed and drained

Olive oil/coconut oil, for cooking

1 sweet potato

1/2 cup red onion, diced

4 tablespoons gluten-free oat flour

2 cloves garlic, minced

2 teaspoons spicy cajun seasoning

1/2 cup cilantro, chopped

1 teaspoon cumin

Sprouts

Salt, to taste

Pepper, to taste

For the Crema:

2 tablespoons cilantro, chopped

1/2 ripe avocado, diced

4 tablespoons low-fat sour cream/plain Greek yogurt 1 teaspoon lime juice

Directions:

1. Rinse quinoa under cold running water. Put a cup of water in a saucepan and heat it. Add quinoa and bring to a boil.

2. Cover, then simmer over low heat until all of the water has absorbed, for about 15 minutes.

3. Turn the heat off and fluff quinoa with a fork. Then transfer quinoa to a bowl and let it cool for 5-10 minutes.

4. Poke potato with a fork and then microwave for a few minutes, until thoroughly cooked and soft. Once cooked, peel the potato and let it cool.

5. Add cooked potato to a food processor along with 1 can black beans, ½ cup chopped cilantro, 2 teaspoons of Cajun seasoning, ½

cup diced onion, 1 teaspoon cumin, and 2 minced cloves of garlic.

Pulse until you obtain a smooth mixture. Transfer it to a bowl and add cooked quinoa.

6. Add in oat flour/oat bran. Mix well and shape into 6 patties. Put patties on a baking sheet and refrigerate for about half an hour.

7. Add all the Crema ingredients to a food processor. Pulse until smooth. Adjust salt to taste and refrigerate.

8. Grease a cooking pan with oil and heat it over medium heat.

Cook each side of patties until light golden, just for 3-4 minutes.

Serve with crema, sprouts, buns, and along with any of your favorite toppings.

Nutrition Info: 206 calories 6 g fat 33.9 g total carbs 7.9 g protein

Coconut Mushroom Soup _Servings: 3_

Cooking Time: 10 Minutes

Ingredients:

1 tablespoon of coconut oil

1 tablespoon of ground ginger

1 cup of cremini mushrooms, chopped

½ teaspoon of turmeric

2 and ½ cups of water

½ cup of canned coconut milk

Sea salt to taste

Directions:

1. Heat-up the coconut oil over medium heat in a large pot, and add the mushrooms. Cook for 3-4 minutes.

2. Put the remaining fixings and boil. Let it simmer for 5 minutes.

3. Divide between three soup bowls, and enjoy!

<u>Nutrition Info:</u> Total Carbohydrates 4g Dietary Fiber: 1g Protein: 2g Total Fat: 14g Calories: 143

Winter Style Fruit Salad Servings: 6

Cooking Time: 0 Minutes

Ingredients:

4 cooked sweet potatoes, cubed (1-inch cubes) 3 pears, cubed (1-inch cubes)

1 cup of grapes, halved

1 apple, cubed

½ cup of pecan halves

2 tablespoons of olive oil

1 tablespoon of red wine vinegar

2 tablespoons of raw honey

Directions:

1. Mix the olive oil, red wine vinegar, then the raw honey to make the dressing, and set aside.

2. Combine the chopped fruit, sweet potato, and pecan halves, and divide this between six serving bowls. Drizzle each bowl with the dressing.

Nutrition Info: Total Carbohydrates 40g Dietary Fiber: 6g Protein: 3g Total Fat: 11g Calories: 251

Honey-roasted Chicken Thighs With Carrots

Servings: 4

Cooking Time: 50 Minutes

Ingredients:

2 tablespoons unsalted butter, at room temperature 3 large carrots, thinly sliced

2 garlic cloves, minced

4 bone-in, skin-on chicken thighs

1 teaspoon salt

½ teaspoon dried rosemary

¼ teaspoon freshly ground black pepper

2 tablespoons honey

1 cup chicken broth or vegetable broth

Lemon wedges, for serving

Directions:

1. Preheat the oven to 400°F. Grease the baking sheet with the butter.

2. Arrange the carrots and garlic in a single layer on the baking sheet.

3. Put the chicken, skin-side up, on top of the vegetables, and season with the salt, rosemary, and pepper.

4. Put the honey on top and add the broth.

5. Roast within 40 to 45 minutes. Remove, then let it rest for 5

minutes, and serve with lemon wedges.

Nutrition Info: Calories 428 Total Fat: 28g Total Carbohydrates: 15g Sugar: 11g Fiber: 2g Protein: 30g Sodium: 732mg

Turkey Chili _Servings: 8_

Cooking Time: 4 Hours And 10 Minutes

Ingredients:

1-pound ground turkey, preferably 99% lean

2 cans of red kidney beans, rinsed & drained (15 oz each) 1 red pepper, chopped

2 cans of tomato sauce (15 oz each)

1 jar deli-sliced tamed jalapeno peppers, drained (16 oz) 2 cans of petite tomatoes, diced (15 oz each) 1 tablespoon cumin

1 yellow pepper, roughly chopped

2 cans of black beans, preferably rinsed & drained (15 oz each) 1 cup corn, frozen

2 tablespoon chili powder

1 tablespoon olive oil

Black pepper & salt to taste

1 medium onion, diced

Green onions, avocado, shredded cheese, Greek yogurt/sour cream, to top, optional

Directions:

1. Warm the oil until hot in a large skillet. Once done, carefully place the turkey into the hot skillet & cook until turn brown. Pour the turkey into the bottom of your slow cooker, preferably 6 quarts.

2. Add the jalapeños, corn, peppers, onion, diced tomatoes, tomato sauce, beans, cumin, and chili powder. Mix, then put pepper and salt to taste.

3. Cover & cook for 6 hours on low heat or 4 hours on high heat.

Serve with the optional toppings and enjoy.

Nutrition Info: kcal 455 Fat: 9 g Fiber: 19 g Protein: 38 g

Lentil Soup With Spices _Servings: 5_

Cooking Time: 25 Minutes

Ingredients:

1 Cup of yellow onion (cut into cubes)

1 Cup of carrot (cut into cubes)

1 Cup of turnip

2tbsp extra-virgin olive oil

2tbsp balsamic vinegar

4 cups of baby spinach

2 cups brown lentils

¼ Cup of fresh parsley

Directions:

1. Preheat the pressure cooker on medium flame and add olive oil and vegetables in it.

2. After 5 minutes, add broth, lentils, and salt in the pot and simmer for 15 minutes.

3. Remove the lid and add spinach and vinegar in it.

4. Stir the soup for 5 minutes and turn off the flame.

5. Garnish it with fresh parsley.

Nutrition Info: Calories 96 Carbs: 16g Fat: 1g Protein: 4g

Garlicky Chicken And Vegetables *Servings: 4*

Cooking Time: 45 Minutes

Ingredients:

2 teaspoons extra-virgin olive oil

1 leek, white part only, thinly sliced

2 large zucchinis, cut into ¼-inch slices

4 bone-in, skin-on chicken breasts

3 garlic cloves, minced

1 teaspoon salt

1 teaspoon dried oregano

¼ teaspoon freshly ground black pepper

½ cup white wine

Juice of 1 lemon

Directions:

1. Preheat the oven to 400°F. Grease the baking sheet with the oil.

2. Place the leek and zucchini on the baking sheet.

3. Put the chicken, skin-side up, and sprinkle with the garlic, salt, oregano, and pepper. Add the wine.

4. Roast within 35 to 40 minutes. Remove and let rest for 5 minutes.

5. Add the lemon juice and serve.

Nutrition Info: Calories 315 Total Fat: 8g Total Carbohydrates: 12g Sugar: 4g Fiber: 2g Protein: 44g Sodium: 685mg

Smoked Salmon Salad *Servings: 4*

Cooking Time: 20 Minutes

Ingredients:

2 baby fennel bulbs, thinly sliced, some fronds reserved 1 tablespoon salted baby capers, rinsed, drained ½ cup natural yogurt

2 tablespoons parsley, chopped

1 tablespoon lemon juice, freshly squeezed

2 tablespoons fresh chives, chopped

1 tablespoon chopped fresh tarragon

180g sliced smoked salmon, low-salt

½ red onion, sliced thinly

1 teaspoon lemon rind, finely grated

½ cup French green lentils, rinsed

60g fresh baby spinach

½ avocado, sliced

A pinch of caster sugar

Directions:

1. Put water in a large saucepan with water and boil over moderate heat. Once boiling; cook the lentils until tender, for 20 minutes; drain well.

2. In the meantime, heat a chargrill pan over high heat in advance.

Spray the fennel slices with some oil & cook until tender, for 2

minutes per side.

3. Process the chives, parsley, yogurt, tarragon, lemon rind, and capers in a food processor until completely smooth and then season with pepper to taste.

4. Place the onion with sugar, juice & a pinch of salt in a large-sized mixing bowl. Set aside for a couple of minutes and then drain.

5. Combine the lentils with onion, fennel, avocado, and spinach in a large-sized mixing bowl. Evenly divide among the plates and then top with the fish. Sprinkle with the leftover fennel fronds & more of fresh parsley. Drizzle with the green goddess dressing. Enjoy.

Nutrition Info: kcal 368 Fat: 14 g Fiber: 8 g Protein: 20 g

Bean Shawarma Salad Servings: 2

Cooking Time: 20 Minutes

Ingredients:

For Preparing Salad

20 Pita chips

5-ounces Spring lettuce

10 Cherry tomatoes

¾ Cup fresh parsley

¼ Cup red onion (chop)

For Chickpeas

1tbsp Olive oil

1 Heading-tbsp cumin and turmeric

½ Heading-tbsp paprika and coriander powder 1 Pinch black pepper

½ Scant Kosher salt

¼tbsp Ginger and cinnamon powder

For Preparing Dressing

3 Garlic Cloves

1tbsp Dried drill

1tbsp Lime juice

Water

½ Cup hummus

Directions:

1. Place a rack in the already preheated oven (204C). Mix chickpeas with all spices and herbs.

2. Place a thin layer of chickpeas on the baking sheet and bake it almost for 20 minutes. Bake it until the beans are golden brown.

3. For preparing the dressing, mix all ingredients in a whisking bowl and blend it. Add water gradually for appropriate smoothness.

4. Mix all herbs and spices for preparing salad.

5. For serving, add pita chips and beans in the salad and drizzle some dressing over it.

Nutrition Info: Calories 173 Carbs: 8g Fat: 6g Protein: 19g

Pineapple Fried Rice *Servings: 4*

Cooking Time: 20 Minutes

Ingredients:

2 carrots, peeled and grated

2 green onions, sliced

3 tablespoons soy sauce

1/2 cup ham, diced

1 tablespoon sesame oil

2 cups canned/fresh pineapple, diced

1/2 teaspoon ginger powder

3 cups brown rice, cooked

1/4 teaspoon white pepper

2 tablespoons olive oil

1/2 cup frozen peas

2 garlic cloves, minced

1/2 cup frozen corn

1 onion, diced

Directions:

1. Put 1 tablespoon sesame oil, 3 tablespoons soy sauce, 2 pinches of white pepper, and 1/2 teaspoon ginger powder in a bowl. Mix well and keep it aside.

2. Preheat oil in a skillet. Add the garlic along with the diced onion.

Cook for about 3-4 minutes, stirring often.

3. Add 1/2 cup frozen peas, grated carrots, and 1/2 cup frozen corn.

Stir until veggies are tender, just for few minutes.

4. Stir in soy sauce mixture, 2 cups of diced pineapple, ½ cup chopped ham, 3 cups cooked brown rice, and sliced green onions.

Cook for about 2-3 minutes, stirring often. Serve!

Nutrition Info: 252 calories 12.8 g fat 33 g total carbs 3 g protein

Lentil Soup Servings: 2

Cooking Time: 30 Minutes

Ingredients:

2 Carrots, medium & diced

2 tbsp. Lemon Juice, fresh

1 tbsp. Turmeric Powder

1/3 cup Lentils, cooked

1 tbsp. Almonds, chopped

1 Celery Stalk, diced

1 bunch of Parsley, chopped freshly

1 Yellow Onion, large & chopped

Black Pepper, freshly grounded

1 Parsnip, medium & chopped

½ tsp. Cumin Powder

3 ½ cups Water

½ tsp. Pink Himalayan Salt

4 kale leaves, chopped roughly

Directions:

1. To start with, place carrots, parsnip, one tablespoon of water and onion in a medium-sized pot over medium heat.

2. Cook the vegetable mixture for 5 minutes while stirring it occasionally.

3. Next, stir in the lentils and spices into it. Combine well.

4. After that, pour water to the pot and bring the mixture to a boil.

5. Now, reduce the heat to low and allow it to simmer for 20 minutes.

6. Off the heat and remove it from the stove. Add the kale, lemon juice, parsley, and salt to it.

7. Then, give a good stir until everything comes together.

8. Top it with almonds and serve it hot.

Nutrition Info: Calories: 242KcalProteins: 10gCarbohydrates: 46gFat: 4g

Delicious Tuna Salad _Servings: 2_

Cooking Time: 15 Minutes

Ingredients:

2 cans tuna packed in water (5oz each), drained ¼ cup mayonnaise

2 tablespoons fresh basil, chopped

1 tablespoon lemon juice, freshly squeezed

2 tablespoons fire-roasted red peppers, chopped ¼ cup kalamata or mixed olives, chopped

2 large vine-ripened tomatoes

1 tablespoon capers

2 tablespoons red onion, minced

Pepper & salt to taste

Directions:

1. Add all the items (except tomatoes) together in a large-sized mixing bowl; give the ingredients a good stir until combined well.

Slice the tomatoes into sixths and then gently pry it open. Scoop the prepared tuna salad mixture into the middle; serve immediately & enjoy.

Nutrition Info: kcal 405 Fat: 24 g Fiber: 3.2 g Protein: 37 g

Aioli With Eggs _Servings: 12_

Cooking Time: 0 Minutes

Ingredients:

2 egg yolks

1 garlic, grated

2 Tbsp. water

½ cup extra virgin olive oil

¼ cup lemon juice, fresh squeezed, pips removed ¼ tsp. sea salt

Dash of cayenne pepper powder

Pinch of white pepper, to taste

Directions:

1. Pour garlic, egg yolks, salt, and water into blender; process until smooth. Put in olive oil in a slow stream until dressing emulsifies.

2. Add in remaining ingredients. Taste; adjust seasoning if needed.

Pour into an airtight container; use as needed.

Nutrition Info: Calories 100 Carbs: 1g Fat: 11g Protein: 0g

Spaghetti Pasta With Herbed Mushroom Sauce

Ingredients:

200 grams/6.3 oz around a large portion of a pack of wheat slender spaghetti *

140 grams cleaned cleaved mushrooms 12-15 pieces*

¼ cup cream

3 cups milk

2 tablespoon cooking olive oil in addition to 2 teaspoon more oil or liquefied margarine to include mid-way 1.5 tablespoon flour

½ cup cleaved onions

¼ to ½ cup crisply ground parmesan cheddar

Couple of bits of dark pepper

Salt to taste

2 teaspoons dried or new thyme *

Bunch of chiffonade new basil leaves

Directions:

1. Cook pasta still somewhat firm as indicated by the bundle.

2. While the pasta is cooking, we should begin making the sauce.

3. Warmth the 3 cups milk in the microwave for 3 minutes or on the stovetop until a stew.

4. At the same time heat 2 tablespoon oil in a non-stick container on medium high and cook the cleaved mushrooms. Cook for around 2 minutes.

5. From the outset the mushrooms will discharge some water, then it will evaporate in the long run and become fresh apiece.

6. Presently lessen the fire to medium include the onions and cook for 1 moment.

7. Presently include 2 teaspoons of softened spread and sprinkle some flour.

8. Mix for 20 seconds.

9. Include the warm milk mixing constantly to shape a smooth sauce.

10. When the sauce thicken i.e. goes to a stew, switch off the fire.

11. Presently include ¼ cup ground parmesan cheddar. Mix until smooth. For 30 seconds.

12. Presently include the salt, pepper and thyme.

13. Give a trial. Modify flavoring if necessary.

14. In interim pasta ought to be bubbled still somewhat firm.

15. Strain the warm water in a colander. Keep the tap running and pour cold water to stop it's cooking, channel all the water and hurl it with the sauce.

16. If not eating promptly, don't blend the pasta in the sauce. Keep the pasta separate, covered with oil and secured.

17. Serve warm with more sprinkle of parmesan cheddar.

Appreciate!

Brown Rice And Shitake Miso Soup With Scallions

Servings: 4

Cooking Time: 45 Minutes

Ingredients:

2 tablespoons sesame oil

1 cup thinly sliced shiitake mushroom caps

1 garlic clove, minced

1 (1½-inch) piece fresh ginger, peeled and sliced 1 cup medium-grain brown rice

½ teaspoon salt

1 tablespoon white miso

2 scallions, thinly sliced

2 tablespoons finely chopped fresh cilantro Directions:

1. Heat-up the oil over medium-high heat in a large pot.

2. Add the mushrooms, garlic, and ginger and sauté until the mushrooms begin to soften about 5 minutes.

3. Put the rice and stir to coat with the oil evenly. Add 2 cups of water and salt and boil.

4. Simmer within 30 to 40 minutes. Use a little of the soup broth to soften the miso, then stir it into the pot until well blended.

5. Mix in the scallions plus cilantro, then serve.

Nutrition Info: Calories 265 Total Fat: 8g Total Carbohydrates: 43g Sugar: 2g Fiber: 3g Protein: 5g Sodium: 456mg

Barbecued Ocean Trout With Garlic And Parsley Dressing

Servings: 8

Cooking Time: 25 Minutes

Ingredients:

3 ½ pounds piece of trout fillet, preferably ocean trout, boned, skin on

4 cloves of garlic, sliced thinly

2 tablespoons capers, coarsely chopped

½ cup flat-leaf parsley leaves, fresh

1 red chili, preferably long; sliced thinly 2 tablespoons lemon juice, freshly squeezed ½ cup olive oil

Lemon wedges, to serve

Directions:

1. Brush the trout with approximately 2 tablespoons of oil; ensure that all sides are coated nicely. Preheat your barbecue over high heat, preferably with a closed hood. Decrease the heat to medium; place the coated trout on the barbecue plate, preferably on the skin-side. Cook until partially cooked

and turn golden, for a couple of minutes. Carefully turn the trout; cook until cooked through, for 12 to 15 minutes, with the hood closed. Transfer the fillet to a large-sized serving platter.

2. In the meantime, heat the leftover oil; garlic over low heat in a small-sized saucepan until just heated through; garlic begins to change its color. Remove, then stir in the capers, lemon juice, chili.

Drizzle the trout with the prepared dressing and then sprinkle with the fresh parsley leaves. Immediately serve with fresh lemon wedges, enjoy.

Nutrition Info: kcal 170 Fat: 30 g Fiber: 2 g Protein: 37 g

Curried Cauliflower And Chickpea Wraps

Ingredients:

1 Ginger Fresh

2 cloves Garlic

1 can Chickpeas

1 Red Onion

8 ounces Cauliflower Florets

1 teaspoon Garam Masala

2 tablespoons Arrowroot Starch

1 Lemon

1 pack Cilantro Fresh

1/4 cup Vegan Yogurt

4 Wraps

3 tablespoons Shredded Coconut

4 ounces Baby Spinach

1 tablespoon Vegetable Oil

1 teaspoon Salt and Pepper To taste

Directions:

1. Preheat the stove to 400 °F (205 °C). Strip and mince 1 tsp of the ginger. Mince the garlic. Channel and wash the chickpeas. Strip and meagerly cut the red onion. Split the lemon.

2. Coat a heating sheet with 1 tbsp vegetable oil. In an enormous bowl, consolidate the minced ginger, garlic, the juice from a large portion of the lemon, chickpeas, cut red onion, cauliflower florets, garam masala, arrowroot starch, and 1/2 tsp salt. Move to the preparing sheet and meal in the broiler until cauliflower is delicate and sautéed in places, around 20 to 25 minutes.

3. Hack the cilantro leaves and delicate stems. In a little bowl, whisk together the cilantro, yogurt, 1 tbsp lemon juice, and a spot of salt and pepper.

4. Spot the encloses by foil and pop them into the stove to warm around 3 to 4 minutes.

5. Spot a little nonstick skillet over medium warmth and include the destroyed coconut. Toast, shaking the dish habitually until daintily cooked, around 2 to 3 minutes.

6. Gap the infant spinach and cooked vegetables between the warm wraps. Lay the cauliflower chickpea wraps on enormous plates and sprinkle with the cilantro sauce.Sprinkle with toasted coconut

Buckwheat Noodle Soup *Servings: 4*

Cooking Time: 25 Minutes

Ingredients:

2 cups Bok Choy, chopped

3 tbsp. Tamari

3 bundles of Buckwheat Noodles

2 cups Edamame Beans

7 oz. Shiitake Mushrooms, chopped

4 cups Water

1 tsp. Ginger, grated

Dash of Salt

1 Garlic Clove, grated

Directions:

1. First, place water, ginger, soy sauce, and garlic in a medium-sized pot over medium heat.

2. Bring the ginger-soy sauce mixture to a boil and then stir in the edamame and shiitake to it.

3. Continue cooking for further 7 minutes or until tender.

4. Next, cook the soba noodles by following the Directions: given in the packet until cooked. Wash and drain well.

5. Now, add the bok choy to shiitake mixture and cook for further one minute or until the bok choy is wilted.

6. Finally, divide the soba noodles among the serving bowls and top it with the mushroom mixture.

Nutrition Info: Calories: 234KcalProteins: 14.2gCarbohydrates: 35.1gFat: 4g

Easy Salmon Salad _Servings: 1_

Cooking Time: 0 Minutes

Ingredients:

1 cup of organic arugula

1 can of wild-caught salmon

½ of an avocado, sliced

1 tablespoon of olive oil

1 teaspoon of Dijon mustard

1 teaspoon of sea salt

Directions:

1. Start by whisking the olive oil, Dijon mustard, and sea salt together in a mixing bowl to make the dressing. Set aside.

2. Assemble the salad with the arugula as the base, and top with the salmon and sliced avocado.

3. Drizzle with the dressing.

Nutrition Info: Total Carbohydrates 7g Dietary Fiber: 5g Protein: 48g Total Fat: 37g Calories: 553

Vegetable Soup *Servings: 4*

Cooking Time: 40 Minutes

Ingredients:

1 tbsp. Coconut Oil

2 cups Kale, chopped

2 Celery Stalks, diced

½ of 15 oz. can of White Beans, drained & rinsed 1 Onion, large & diced

¼ tsp. Black Pepper

1 Carrot, medium & diced

2 cups Cauliflower, cut into florets

1 tsp. Turmeric, grounded

1 tsp. Sea Salt

3 Garlic cloves, minced

6 cups Vegetable Broth

Directions:

1. To start with, heat oil in a large pot over medium-low heat.

2. Stir in the onion to the pot and sauté it for 5 minutes or until softened.

3. Put the carrot plus celery to the pot and continue cooking for another 4 minutes or until the veggies softened.

4. Now, spoon in the turmeric, garlic, and ginger to the mixture. Stir well.

5. Cook the veggie mixture for 1 minute or until fragrant.

6. Then, pour the vegetable broth along with salt and pepper and bring the mixture to a boil.

7. Once it starts boiling, add the cauliflower. Reduce the heat and simmer the vegetable mixture for 13 to 15 minutes or until the cauliflower is softened.

8. Finally, add the beans and kale—Cook within 2 minutes.

9. Serve it hot.

Nutrition Info: Calories 192Kcal Proteins:12.6g Carbohydrates: 24.6g Fat: 6.4g

Lemony Garlic Shrimp <u>*Servings: 4*</u>

Cooking Time: 15 Minutes

Ingredients:

1 and ¼ pounds shrimp, boiled or steamed

3 tablespoons garlic, minced

¼ cup lemon juice

2 tablespoons olive oil

¼ cup parsley

Directions:

1. Take a small skillet and place it over medium heat, add garlic and oil and stir cook for 1 minute.

2. Add parsley, lemon juice and season with salt and pepper accordingly.

3. Add shrimp in a large bowl and transfer the mixture from the skillet over the shrimp.

4. Chill and serve.

<u>Nutrition Info:</u> Calories: 130Fat: 3gCarbohydrates: 2gProtein: 22g

Blt Spring Rolls Ingredients:

new lettuce, torn pieces or slashed

avocado cuts, discretionary

SESAME-SOY DIPPING SAUCE

1/4 cup Soy Sauce

1/4 cup cold water

1 Tablespoon Mayonnaise (discretionary, this makes the plunge velvety)

1 teaspoon new Lime Juice

1 teaspoon Sesame Oil

1 teaspoon sriracha sauce or any hot sauce (discretionary) Directions:

1. medium tomato (seeded and cut 1/4" thick) 2. pieces bacon, cooked

3. new basil, mint or different herbs

4. rice paper

Brisket With Blue Cheese _Servings: 6_

Cooking Time: 8 Hrs. 10 Minutes

Ingredients:

1 cup of water

1/2 tbsp garlic paste

1/4 cup soy sauce

1 ½ lb. corned beef brisket

1/3 teaspoon ground coriander

1/4 teaspoon cloves, ground

1 tbsp olive oil

1 shallot, chopped

2 oz. blue cheese, crumbled

Cooking spray

Directions:

1. Place a pan over moderate heat and add oil to heat.

2. Toss in shallots and stir and cook for 5 minutes.

3. Stir in garlic paste and cook for 1 minute.

4. Transfer it to the slow cooker, greased with cooking spray.

5. Place brisket in the same pan and sear until golden from both sides.

6. Transfer the beef to the slow cooker along with other ingredients except for cheese.

7. Put on its lid and cook for 8 hrs. on low heat.

8. Garnish with cheese and serve.

Nutrition Info: Calories 397, Protein 23.5g, Fat 31.4g, Carbs 3.9g, Fiber 0 g

Cold Soba With Miso Dressing Ingredients:

6oz buckwheat Soba noodles

1/2 cups destroyed carrots

1 cup solidified shelled edamame, defrosted 2 Persian cucumbers, cut

1 cup hacked cilantro

1/4 cup sesame seeds

2 tbsp dark sesame seeds

White Miso Dressing (makes 2 cups)

2/3 cup white miso glue

Juice of 2 medium size lemons

4 tbsp rice vinegar

4 tbsp additional virgin olive oil

4 tbsp squeezed orange

2 tbsp new ground ginger

2 tbsp maple syrup

Directions:

1. Cook soba noodles as per the guidelines in the bundling (make a point not to overcook them or they will get sticky and remain together). Channel well and move to an enormous bowl 2. Include destroyed carrots, edamame, cucumber, cilantro and sesame seeds

3. To set up the dressing, consolidate every one of the fixings in a blender. Mix until smooth

4. Pour wanted measure of dressing over the noodles (we utilized about a cup and a half)

Baked Buffalo Cauliflower Chunks *Servings: 2*

Cooking Time: 35 Minutes

Ingredients:

¼-cup water

¼-cup banana flour

A pinch of salt and pepper

1-pc medium cauliflower, cut into bite-size pieces ½-cup hot sauce

2-Tbsp.s butter, melted

Blue cheese or ranch dressing (optional)

Directions:

1. Preheat your oven to 425°F. Meanwhile, line a baking pan with foil.

2. Combine the water, flour, and a pinch of salt and pepper in a large mixing bowl.

3. Mix well until thoroughly combined.

4. Add the cauliflower; toss to coat thoroughly.

5. Transfer the mixture to the baking pan. Bake for 15 minutes, flipping once.

6. While baking, combine the hot sauce and butter in a small bowl.

7. Pour the sauce over the baked cauliflower.

8. Return the baked cauliflower to the oven, and bake further for 20 minutes.

9. Serve immediately with a ranch dressing on the side, if desired.

Nutrition Info: Calories: 168Cal Fat: 5.6gProtein: 8.4gCarbs: 23.8gFiber: 2.8g

Garlic Chicken Bake With Basil &tomatoes

Servings: 4

Cooking Time: 30 Minutes

Ingredients:

½ medium yellow onion

2tbsp Olive oil

3 Minced Garlic Cloves

1 Cup Basil (loosely cut)

1.lb Boneless chicken breast

14.5-ounces Italian chop tomatoes

Salt & pepper

4 Medium zucchinis (spiralized into noodles) 1tbsp crushed red pepper

2tbsp Olive oil

Directions:

1. Pound the chicken pieces with a pan for fast cooking. Sprinkle salt, pepper, and oil on chicken pieces and marinate both sides of chicken equally.

2. Fry chicken pieces on a large hot skillet for 2-3 minutes on each side.

3. Sautee onion in the same skillet pan until it's brown. Add tomatoes, basil leaves, and garlic in it.

4. Simmer it for 3 minutes and add all spices and chicken in the skillet.

5. Serve it on the plate along with saucy zoodles.

<u>Nutrition Info:</u> Calories 44 Carbs: 7g Fat: 0g Protein: 2g

Creamy Turmeric Cauliflower Soup *Servings: 4*

Cooking Time: 15 Minutes

Ingredients:

2 tablespoons extra-virgin olive oil

1 leek, white part only, thinly sliced

3 cups cauliflower florets

1 garlic clove, peeled

1 (1¼-inch) piece fresh ginger, peeled and sliced 1½ teaspoons turmeric

½ teaspoon salt

¼ teaspoon freshly ground black pepper

¼ teaspoon ground cumin

3 cups vegetable broth

1 cup full-Fat: coconut milk

¼ cup finely chopped fresh cilantro

Directions:

1. Heat-up the oil over high heat in a large pot.

2. Sauté the leek within 3 to 4 minutes.

3. Put the cauliflower, garlic, ginger, turmeric, salt, pepper, and cumin and sauté for 1 to 2 minutes.

4. Put the broth, and boil.

5. Simmer within 5 minutes.

6. Purée the soup using an immersion blender until smooth.

7. Stir in the coconut milk and cilantro, heat through, and serve.

Nutrition Info: Calories 264 Total Fat: 23g Total Carbohydrates: 12g Sugar: 5g Fiber: 4g Protein: 7g Sodium: 900mg

Mushroom, Kale, And Sweet Potato Brown Rice

Servings: 4

Cooking Time: 50 Minutes

Ingredients:

¼ cup extra-virgin olive oil

4 cups coarsely chopped kale leaves

2 leeks, white parts only, thinly sliced

1 cup sliced mushrooms

2 garlic cloves, minced

2 cups peeled sweet potatoes cut into ½-inch dice 1 cup of brown rice

2 cups vegetable broth

1 teaspoon salt

¼ teaspoon freshly ground black pepper

¼ cup freshly squeezed lemon juice

2 tablespoons finely chopped fresh flat-leaf parsley Directions:

1. Heat the oil over high heat.

2. Add the kale, leeks, mushrooms, and garlic and sauté until soft, about 5 minutes.

3. Add the sweet potatoes and rice and sauté for about 3 minutes.

4. Add the broth, salt, and pepper and boil. Simmer within 30 to 40 minutes.

5. Combine in the lemon juice and parsley, then serve.

<u>Nutrition Info:</u> Calories 425 Fat: 15g Total Carbohydrates: 65g Sugar: 6g Fiber: 6g Protein: 11g Sodium: 1045mg

Baked Tilapia Recipe With Pecan Rosemary Topping

Servings: 4

Cooking Time: 20 Minutes

Ingredients:

4 tilapia fillets (4 ounces each)

½ teaspoon brown sugar or coconut palm sugar 2 teaspoons fresh rosemary, chopped

1/3 cup raw pecans, chopped

A pinch of cayenne pepper

1 ½ teaspoon olive oil

1 large egg white

1/8 teaspoon salt

1/3 cup panko breadcrumbs, preferably whole-wheat Directions:

1. Heat-up your oven to 350 F.

2. Stir the pecans with breadcrumbs, coconut palm sugar, rosemary, cayenne pepper, and salt in a small-sized baking dish. Add the olive oil; toss.

3. Bake within 7 to 8 minutes, until the mixture turns light golden brown.

4. Adjust the heat to 400 F and coat a large-sized glass baking dish with some cooking spray.

5. Whisk the egg white in the shallow dish. Work in batches; dip the fish (one tilapia at a time) into the egg white, and then, coating lightly into the pecan mixture. Put the coated fillets in the baking dish.

6. Press the leftover pecan mixture over the tilapia fillets.

7. Bake within 8 to 10 minutes. Serve immediately & enjoy.

Nutrition Info: kcal 222 Fat: 10 g Fiber: 2 g Protein: 27 g

Black Bean Tortilla Wrap *Servings: 2*

Cooking Time: 0 Minutes

Ingredients:

¼ cup of corn

1 handful of fresh basil

½ cup of arugula

1 tablespoon of nutritional yeast

¼ cup of canned black beans

1 peach, sliced

1 teaspoon of lime juice

2 gluten-free tortillas

Directions:

1. Divide the beans, corn, arugula, and peaches between the two tortillas.

2. Top each tortilla with half the fresh basil and lime juice Nutrition Info: Total Carbohydrates 44g Dietary Fiber: 7g Protein: 8g Total Fat: 1g Calories: 203

White Bean Chicken With Winter Green Vegetables

Servings: 8

Cooking Time: 45 Minutes

Ingredients:

4 Garlic cloves

1tbsp Olive oil

3 medium parsnips

1kg Small cubes of chicken

1 Teaspoon cumin powder

2 Leaks & 1 Green part

2 Carrots (cut into cubes)

1 ¼ White kidney beans (overnight soaked)

½ Teaspoon dried oregano

2 Teaspoon Kosher salt

Cilantro leaves

1 1/2tbsp Ground ancho chilies

Directions:

1. Cook garlic, leeks, chicken, and olive oil in a large pot on a medium flame for 5 minutes.

2. Now add carrots and parsnips, and after stirring for 2 minutes, add all seasoning ingredients.

3. Stir until the fragrant starts coming from it.

4. Now add beans and 5 cups of water in the pot.

5. Bring it to a boil and reduce the flame.

6. Allow it to simmer almost for 30 minutes and garnish with parsley and cilantro leaves.

Nutrition Info: Calories 263 Carbs: 24g Fat: 7g Protein: 26g

Herbed Baked Salmon Servings: 2

Cooking Time: 15 Minutes

Ingredients:

10 oz. Salmon Fillet

1 tsp. Olive Oil

1 tsp. Honey

1 tsp. Tarragon, fresh

1/8 tsp. Salt

2 tsp. Dijon Mustard

¼ tsp. Thyme, dried

¼ tsp. Oregano, dried

Directions:

1. Preheat the oven to 425 ° F.

2. After that, combine all the ingredients, excluding the salmon in a medium-sized bowl.

3. Now, spoon this mixture evenly over the salmon.

4. Then, place the salmon with the skin side down on the parchment paper-lined baking sheet.

5. Finally, bake for 8 minutes or until the fish flakes.

Nutrition Info: Calories: 239KcalProteins: 31gCarbohydrates: 3gFat: 11g

Greek Yogurt Chicken Salad

Ingredients:

Chopped chicken

Green apple

Red onion

Celery

Dried cranberries

Directions:

1. Greek yogurt chicken serving of mixed greens is such an extraordinary supper prep lunch thought. You can place it in an artisan jostle and eat only that or you can pack it in a super prep compartment with more veggies, chips, and so forth. Here are some serving recommendations.

2. On a bit of toast

3. In a tortilla with lettuce

4. With chips or saltines

5. In a bit of ice burg lettuce (low carb choice!)

Pounded Chickpea Salad

Ingredients:

1 avocado

1/2 crisp lemon

1 can chickpeas depleted (19 oz)

1/4 cup cut red onion

2 cups grape tomatoes cut

2 cups diced cucumber

1/2 cup crisp parsley

3/4 cup diced green chime pepper

Dressing

1/4 cup olive oil

2 tablespoons red wine vinegar

1/2 teaspoon cumin

salt and pepper

Directions:

1. Cut avocado into 3D squares and spot in bowl. Press the juice from 1/2 lemon over the avocado and delicately mix to consolidate.

2. Include remaining serving of mixed greens ingredients and delicately hurl to join.

3. Refrigerate at any rate one hour before serving.

Valencia Salad Servings: 10

Cooking Time: 0 Minutes

Ingredients:

1 tsp. Kalamata olives in oil, pitted, drained lightly, halved, julienned

1 head, small Romaine lettuce, rinsed, spun-dried, sliced into bite-sized pieces

½ piece, small shallot, julienned

1 tsp. Dijon mustard

½ small satsuma or tangerine, pulp only

1 tsp. white wine vinegar

1 tsp. extra virgin olive oil

1 pinch fresh thyme, minced

Pinch of sea salt

Pinch of black pepper, to taste

Directions:

1. Combine vinegar, oil, fresh thyme, salt, mustard, black pepper, and honey, if using. Whisk well until dressing emulsifies a little.

2. Toss together the remaining salad ingredients in a salad bowl.

3. Drizzle dressing on top when about to serve. Serve immediately with 1 slice if sugar-free sourdough bread or saltine.

Nutrition Info: Calories 238 Carbs: 23g Fat: 15g Protein: 8g

"Eat Your Greens" Soup <u>Servings: 4</u>

Cooking Time: 20 Minutes

Ingredients:

¼ cup extra-virgin olive oil

2 leeks, white parts only, thinly sliced

1 fennel bulb, trimmed and thinly sliced

1 garlic clove, peeled

1 bunch Swiss chard, coarsely chopped

4 cups coarsely chopped kale

4 cups coarsely chopped mustard greens

3 cups vegetable broth

2 tablespoons apple cider vinegar

1 teaspoon salt

¼ teaspoon freshly ground black pepper

¼ cup chopped cashews (optional)

Directions:

1. Heat-up the oil over high heat in a large pot.

2. Add the leeks, fennel, and garlic and sauté until softened, for about 5 minutes.

3. Add the Swiss chard, kale, and mustard greens and sauté until the greens wilt, 2 to 3 minutes.

4. Put the broth and boil.

5. Simmer within 5 minutes.

6. Stir in the vinegar, salt, pepper, and cashews (if using).

7. Purée the soup using an immersion blender until smooth and serve.

Nutrition Info: Calories 238 Total Fat: 14g Total Carbohydrates: 22g Sugar: 4g Fiber: 6g Protein: 9g Sodium: 1294mg

Miso Salmon And Green Beans Servings: 4

Cooking Time: 25 Minutes

Ingredients:

1 tablespoon sesame oil

1-pound green beans, trimmed

1-pound skin-on salmon fillets, cut into 4 steaks ¼ cup white miso

2 teaspoons gluten-free tamari or soy sauce 2 scallions, thinly sliced

Directions:

1. Preheat the oven to 400°F. Grease the baking sheet with the oil.

2. Put the green beans, then the salmon on top of the green beans, and brush each piece with the miso.

3. Roast within 20 to 25 minutes.

4. Drizzle with the tamari, sprinkle with the scallions, and serve.

Nutrition Info: Calories 213 Total Fat: 7g Total Carbohydrates: 13g Sugar: 3g Fiber: 5g Protein: 27g Sodium: 989mg

Leek, Chicken, And Spinach Soup Servings: 4

Cooking Time: 15 Minutes

Ingredients:

3 tablespoons unsalted butter

2 leeks, white parts only, thinly sliced

4 cups baby spinach

4 cups chicken broth

1 teaspoon salt

¼ teaspoon freshly ground black pepper

2 cups shredded rotisserie chicken

1 tablespoon thinly sliced fresh chives

2 teaspoons grated or minced lemon zest

Directions:

1. Dissolve the butter over high heat in a large pot.

2. Add the leeks and sauté until softened and beginning to brown, 3

to 5 minutes.

3. Add the spinach, broth, salt, and pepper and boil.

4. Simmer within 1 to 2 minutes.

5. Put the chicken and cook within 1 to 2 minutes.

6. Sprinkle with the chives and lemon zest and serve.

Nutrition Info: Calories 256 Total Fat: 12g Total Carbohydrates: 9g Sugar: 3g Fiber: 2g Protein: 27g Sodium: 1483mg

Dark Choco Bombs Servings: 24

Cooking Time: 5 Minutes

Ingredients:

1 cup heavy cream

1 cup cream cheese softened

1 teaspoon vanilla essence

1/2 cup dark chocolate

2 oz. Stevia

Directions:

1. Melt chocolate in a bowl by heating in a microwave.

2. Beat the rest of the ingredients in a mixer until fluffy, then stir in the chocolate melt.

3. Mix well, then divide the mixture in a muffin tray lined with muffin cups.

4. Refrigerate for 3 hrs.

5. Serve.

Nutrition Info: Calories 97 Fat 5 g, Carbs 1 g, Protein 1 g, Fiber 0 g

Italian Stuffed Peppers _Servings: 6_

Cooking Time: 40 Minutes

Ingredients:

1 teaspoon garlic powder

1/2 cup mozzarella, shredded

1 lb. lean ground meat

1/2 cup parmesan cheese

3 bell peppers, cut into half lengthwise, stems, seeds and ribs removed

1 (10 oz.) package frozen spinach

2 cups marinara sauce

1/2 teaspoon salt

1 teaspoon Italian seasoning

Directions:

1. Coat a foil-lined baking sheet with non-stick spray. Place the peppers on the baking pan.

2. Add turkey to a non-stick pan and cook over medium heat until no longer pink.

3. When almost cooked, add 2 cups of marinara sauce and seasonings— Cook for about 8-10 minutes.

4. Add spinach along with 1/2 cup parmesan cheese. Stir until well-combined.

5. Add half cup of the meat mixture into each pepper and divide cheese among all—Preheat the oven to 450 F.

6. Bake peppers for about 25-30 minutes. Cool, and serve.

Nutrition Info: 150 calories 2 g fat 11 g total carbs 20 g protein

Smoked Trout Wrapped In Lettuce Servings: 4

Cooking Time: 45 Minutes

Ingredients:

¼ Cup salt-roasted potatoes

1 cup grape tomatoes

½ Cup basil leaves

16 small & medium size lettuce leaves

1/3 cup Asian sweet chili

2 Carrots

1/3 Cup Shallots (thin sliced)

¼ Cup thin slice Jalapenos

1tbsp Sugar

2-4.5 Ounces skinless smoked trout

2tbsp Fresh lime Juice

1 Cucumber

Directions:

1. Cut carrots and cucumber in slim strip size.

2. Marinate these vegetables for 20 mins with sugar, fish sauce, lime juice, shallots, and jalapeno.

3. Add trout pieces and other herbs in this vegetable mixture and blend.

4. Strain water from vegetable and trout mixture and again toss it to blend.

5. Place lettuce leaves on a plate and transfer trout salad on them.

6. Garnish this salad with peanuts and chili sauce.

Nutrition Info: Calories 180 Carbs: 0g Fat: 12g Protein: 18g

Devilled Egg Salad Ingredients:

12 enormous eggs

1/4 cup slashed green onion

1/2 cup slashed celery

1/2 cup slashed red chime pepper

2 tablespoons Dijon mustard

1/3 cup mayonnaise

1 tablespoon juice, white wine or sherry vinegar 1/4 teaspoon Tabasco or other hot sauce (pretty much to taste) 1/2 teaspoon paprika (pretty much to taste) 1/2 teaspoon dark pepper (pretty much to taste) 1/4 teaspoon salt (more to taste)

Directions:

1. Hard heat up the eggs: The simplest method to make hard bubbled eggs that are anything but difficult to strip is to steam them.

Fill a pan with 1 inch of water and addition a steamer bushel. (On the off chance that you don't have a steamer bushel, that is alright.) 2. Heat the water to the point of boiling, delicately place the eggs in the steamer bin or straightforwardly in the pan. Spread the pot. Set your clock for 15 minutes. Evacuate eggs and set in frigid virus water to cool.

3. Prep the eggs and veggies: Chop the eggs coarsely and put them into a huge bowl. Include the green onion, celery, and red chime pepper.

4. Make the plate of mixed greens: In little bowl, combine the mayo, mustard, vinegar, and Tabasco. Tenderly mix the mayo dressing into the bowl with the eggs and vegetables. Include the paprika and salt and dark pepper. Change seasonings to taste.

Sesame-tamari Baked Chicken With Green Beans

Servings: 4

Cooking Time: 45 Minutes

Ingredients:

1-pound green beans, trimmed

4 bone-in, skin-on chicken breasts

2 tablespoons honey

1 tablespoon sesame oil

1 tablespoon gluten-free tamari or soy sauce 1 cup chicken or vegetable broth

Directions:

1. Preheat the oven to 400°F.

2. Arrange the green beans on a large rimmed baking sheet.

3. Put the chicken, skin-side up, on top of the beans.

4. Drizzle with the honey, oil, and tamari. Add the broth.

5. Roast within 35 to 40 minutes. Remove, let it rest for 5 minutes and serve.

Nutrition Info: Calories 378 Total Fat: 10g Total Carbohydrates: 19g Sugar: 10g Fiber: 4g Protein: 54g Sodium: 336mg

Ginger Chicken Stew *Servings: 6*

Cooking Time: 20 Minutes

Ingredients:

¼ cup chicken thigh fillet, diced

¼ cup cooked egg noodles

1 unripe papaya, peeled, diced

1 cup chicken broth, low-sodium, low-fat

1 medallion ginger, peeled, crushed

dash onion powder

dash garlic powder, add more if desired

1 cup of water

1 tsp. fish sauce

dash white pepper

1-piece, small bird's eye chili, minced

Directions:

1. Put all the fixing in a large Dutch oven set over high heat. Boil.

Turn down heat to the lowest setting. Put the lid on.

2. Let the stew cook for 20 minutes or until papaya is fork-tender.

Turn off heat. Consume as is, or with ½ cup of cooked rice. Serve warm.

Nutrition Info: Calories 273 Carbs: 15g Fat: 9g Protein: 33g

Creamy Garbano Salad Ingredients:

Plate of mixed greens

2 14 oz jars Chickpeas

3/4 cup Carrot little shakers

3/4 cup Celery little shakers

3/4 cup Bell Pepper Small shakers

1 Scallion hacked

1/4 cup Red Onion little shakers

1/2 Large Avocado

6 oz smooth tofu

1 Tbsp Apple Cider Vinegar

1 Tbsp Lemon Juice

1 Tbsp Dijon Mustard

1 Tbsp Sweet Relish

1/4 tsp Smoked Paprika

1/4 tsp Celery seeds

1/4 tsp Black Pepper

1/4 tsp Mustard powder

Ocean salt to taste

Sandwich Fix'ns

Grown Whole Grain Bread

Cut Roma Tomatoes

Spread Lettuce

Directions:

1. Get ready and slash your carrots, celery, chime pepper, red onion and scallion and spot in a little blending bowl. Put In a safe spot.

2. Utilizing a little submersion blender or nourishment processor, mix the avocado, tofu, apple juice vinegar, lemon juice, and mustard until smooth.

3. Strain and wash your garbanzos, and spot in a medium blending bowl. With a potato masher or a fork squash the beans until most are separated and it begins to take after fish plate of mixed greens. You don't need it to be smooth however finished and stout. Season the beans with a spot of salt and pepper.

4. Include the cleaved vegetables, avocado-tofu cream, and the rest of the flavors and relish and blend well. Taste and alter as indicated by your inclination.

Carrot Noodles With Ginger Lime Peanut Sauce

Ingredients:

For the carrot pasta:

5 huge carrots, stripped and julienned or spiraled into slim strips 1/3 cup (50g) cooked cashews

2 tablespoons new cilantro, finely hacked

For the ginger-peanut sauce:

2 tablespoons rich nutty spread

4 tablespoons ordinary coconut milk

Squeeze cayenne pepper

2 huge cloves garlic, finely hacked

1 tablespoon new ginger, stripped and ground 1 tablespoon lime juice

Salt, to taste

Directions:

1. Consolidate all sauce ingredients in a little bowl and combine until smooth and rich and put in a safe spot while you julienne/spiralize the carrots.

2. In a huge serving bowl, tenderly hurl the carrots and sauce together until equally covered. Top with broiled cashews (or peanuts) and newly hacked cilantro.

Roasted Vegetables With Sweet Potatoes And White Beans

Servings: 4

Cooking Time: 25 Minutes

Ingredients:

2 small sweet potatoes, dice

½ red onion, cut into ¼-inch dice

1 medium carrot, peeled and thinly sliced

4 ounces green beans, trimmed

¼ cup extra-virgin olive oil

1 teaspoon salt

¼ teaspoon freshly ground black pepper

1 (15½-ounce) can white beans, drained and rinsed 1 tablespoon minced or grated lemon zest

1 tablespoon chopped fresh dill

Directions:

1. Preheat the oven to 400°F.

2. Combine the sweet potatoes, onion, carrot, green beans, oil, salt, and pepper on a large rimmed baking sheet and mix to combine well. Arrange in a single layer.

3. Roast until the vegetables are tender, 20 to 25 minutes.

4. Add the white beans, lemon zest, and dill, mix well and serve.

Nutrition Info: Calories 315 Total Fat: 13g Total Carbohydrates: 42g Sugar: 5g Fiber: 13g Protein: 10g Sodium: 632mg

Kale Salad _Servings: 1_

Cooking Time: 0 Minutes

Ingredients:

1 cup of fresh kale

½ cup of blueberries

½ cup of pitted cherries halved

¼ cup of dried cranberries

1 tablespoon of sesame seeds

2 tablespoons of olive oil

Juice of 1 lemon

Directions:

1. Combine the olive oil and lemon juice, then toss the kale in the dressing.

2. Put the kale leaves into a salad bowl, and top with the fresh blueberries, cherries, and cranberries.

3. Top with the sesame seeds.

Nutrition Info: Total Carbohydrates 48g Dietary Fiber: 7g Protein: 6g Total Fat: 33g Calories: 477

Coconut And Hazelnut Chilled Glass Servings: 1

Cooking Time: 0 Minute

Ingredients:

½ cup coconut almond milk

¼ cup hazelnuts, chopped

1 and ½ cups water

1 pack stevia

Directions:

1. Add listed Ingredients to the blender

2. Blend until you have a smooth and creamy texture 3. Serve chilled and enjoy!

Nutrition Info: Calories: 457Fat: 46gCarbohydrates: 12gProtein: 7g

Cool Garbanzo And Spinach Beans Servings: 4

Cooking Time: 0 Minute

Ingredients:

1 tablespoon olive oil

½ onion, diced

10 ounces spinach, chopped

12 ounces garbanzo beans

½ teaspoon cumin

Directions:

1. Take a skillet and add olive oil, let it warm over medium-low heat 2. Add onions, garbanzo and cook for 5 minutes 3. Stir in spinach, cumin, garbanzo beans and season with salt 4. Use a spoon to smash gently

5. Cook thoroughly until heated, enjoy!

Nutrition Info: Calories: 90Fat: 4gCarbohydrates: 11gProtein: 4g

Taro Leaves In Coconut Sauce Servings: 5

Cooking Time: 20 Minutes

Ingredients:

4 cups dried taro leaves

2 cans of coconut cream, divided

¼ cup ground pork, 90% lean

1 tsp. shrimp paste

1 bird's eye chili, minced

Directions:

1. Except for 1 can of coconut cream, place all ingredients in a crockpot set at medium setting. Secure lid. Cook undisturbed for 3 to 3½ hours.

2. Pour the remaining can of coconut cream before turning off the heat. Stir and serve.

Nutrition Info: Calories 264 Carbs: 8g Fat: 24g Protein: 4g

Roasted Tofu And Greens Servings: 4

Cooking Time: 20 Minutes

Ingredients:

3 cups baby spinach or kale

1 tablespoon sesame oil

1 tablespoon ginger, minced

1 garlic clove, minced

1-pound firm tofu, cut into 1-inch dice

1 tablespoon gluten-free tamari or soy sauce ¼ teaspoon red pepper flakes (optional)

1 teaspoon rice vinegar

2 scallions, thinly sliced

Directions:

1. Preheat the oven to 400°F.

2. Combine the spinach, oil, ginger, and garlic on a large rimmed baking sheet.

3. Bake until the spinach has wilted, 3 to 5 minutes.

4. Add the tofu, tamari, and red pepper flakes (if using) and toss to combine well.

5. Bake until the tofu is beginning to brown, 10 to 15 minutes.

6. Top with the vinegar and scallions and serve.

Nutrition Info: Calories 121 Total Fat: 8g Total Carbohydrates: 4g Sugar: 1g Fiber: 2g Protein: 10g Sodium: 258mg

Meatball Taco Bowls Ingredients:

Meatballs:

1 lb. Lean Ground Beef (sub any ground meat like pork, turkey or chicken)

1 Egg

1/4 cup finely cleaved Kale or crisp herbs like Parsley or Cilantro (discretionary)

1 tsp Salt

1/2 tsp Black Pepper

Taco Bowls

2 cups Enchilada Sauce (we utilize custom made) 16 Meatballs (fixings recorded previously)

2 cups Cooked Rice, white or dark colored

1 Avocado, cut

1 cup locally acquired Salsa or Pico de Gallo 1 cup Shredded Cheese

1 Jalapeno, daintily cut (discretionary)

1 Tbsp Cilantro, cleaved

1 Lime, cut into wedges

Tortilla Chips, for serving

Directions:

1. To Make/Freeze

2. In a huge bowl, join ground meat, eggs, kale (if utilizing), salt and pepper. Blend in with your hands just until equitably consolidated.

Structure into 16 meatballs around 1-inch in distance across and place on a sheet dish fixed with foil.

3. In the event that utilizing inside several days, refrigerate for as long as 2 days.

4. In the event that freezing, place sheet container in cooler until meatballs are strong. Move to a cooler sack. Meatballs will keep in the cooler for 3 to 4 months.

5. To Cook

6. In a medium pot, bring enchilada sauce to a low stew. Include meatballs (no compelling reason to defrost first if meatballs were

solidified). Stew meatballs until cooked through, 12 minutes assuming crisp and 20 minutes whenever solidified.

7. While meatballs stew, prep different fixings.

8. Amass taco bowls by garnish rice with meatballs and sauce, cut avocado, salsa, cheddar, jalapeño cuts, and cilantro. Present with lime wedges and tortilla chips.

Avocado Pesto Zoodles With Salmon *Servings: 4*

Cooking Time: 25 Minutes

Ingredients:

1 tablespoon pesto

1 lemon

2 frozen/fresh salmon steaks

1 large zucchini, spiralized

1 tablespoon black pepper

1 avocado

1/4 cup parmesan, grated

Italian seasoning

Directions:

1. Heat-up the oven to 375 F. Season salmon with Italian seasoning, salt, and pepper and bake for 20 minutes.

2. Add avocados to the bowl along with a tablespoon of pepper, lemon juice, and a tablespoon of pesto. Mash the avocados and keep it aside.

3. Add zucchini noodles to a serving platter, followed by avocado mixture and salmon.

4. Sprinkle with cheese. Add more pesto if needed. Enjoy!

Nutrition Info: 128 calories 9.9 g fat 9 g total carbs 4 g protein

Turmeric-spiced Sweet Potatoes, Apple, And Onion With Chicken

Servings: 4

Cooking Time: 45 Minutes

Ingredients:

2 tablespoons unsalted butter, at room temperature 2 medium sweet potatoes

1 large Granny Smith apple

1 medium onion, thinly sliced

4 bone-in, skin-on chicken breasts

1 teaspoon salt

1 teaspoon turmeric

1 teaspoon dried sage

¼ teaspoon freshly ground black pepper

1 cup apple cider, white wine, or chicken broth Directions:

1. Preheat the oven to 400°F. Grease the baking sheet with the butter.

2. Arrange the sweet potatoes, apple, and onion in a single layer on the baking sheet.

3. Put the chicken, skin-side up, and season with the salt, turmeric, sage, and pepper. Add the cider.

4. Roast within 35 to 40 minutes. Remove, let it rest for 5 minutes and serve.

Nutrition Info: Calories 386 Total Fat: 12g Total Carbohydrates: 26g Sugar: 10g Fiber: 4g Protein: 44g Sodium: 932mg

Seared Herbed Salmon Steak *Servings: 4*

Cooking Time: 5 Minutes

Ingredients:

1 lb. salmon steak, rinsed 1/8 tsp cayenne pepper 1 tsp chili powder

½ tsp cumin

2 garlic cloves, minced

1 tablespoon olive oil

¾ tsp salt

1 tsp freshly ground black pepper

Directions:

1. Preheat the oven to 350 degrees F.

2. In a bowl, combine cayenne pepper, chili powder, cumin, salt, and black pepper. Set aside.

3. Drizzle in olive oil onto the salmon steak. Rub on both sides. Rub garlic and the prepared spice mixture. Let sit for 10 minutes.

4. After allowing the flavors to meld, prepare an ovenproof skillet.

Heat the olive oil. Once hot, season the salmon for 4 minutes on both sides.

5. Transfer skillet inside the oven. Bake for 10 minutes. Serve.

Nutrition Info: Calories 210 Carbs: 0g Fat: 14g Protein: 19g

Tofu And Italian-seasoned Summer Vegetables

Servings: 4

Cooking Time: 20 Minutes

Ingredients:

2 large zucchinis, cut into ¼-inch slices

2 large summer squash, cut into ¼-inch-thick slices 1-pound firm tofu, cut into 1-inch dice

1 cup vegetable broth or water

3 tablespoons extra-virgin olive oil

2 garlic cloves, sliced

1 teaspoon salt

1 teaspoon Italian herb seasoning blend

¼ teaspoon freshly ground black pepper

1 tablespoon thinly sliced fresh basil

Directions:

1. Preheat the oven to 400°F.

2. Combine the zucchini, squash, tofu, broth, oil, garlic, salt, Italian herb seasoning blend, and pepper on a large rimmed baking sheet, and mix well.

3. Roast within 20 minutes.

4. Sprinkle with the basil and serve.

Nutrition Info: Calories 213 Total Fat: 16g Total Carbohydrates: 9g Sugar: 4g Fiber: 3g Protein: 13g Sodium: 806mg

Strawberry And Goat Cheese Salad Ingredients:

1-pound crisp strawberries, diced

Discretionary: 1 to 2 teaspoons nectar or maple syrup, to taste 2 ounces disintegrated goat cheddar (about ½ cup) ¼ cup cleaved crisp basil, in addition to a couple of little basil leaves for embellish

1 tablespoon extra-virgin olive oil

1 tablespoon thick balsamic vinegar*

½ teaspoon Maldon flaky ocean salt or an inadequate ¼

teaspoon fine ocean salt

Crisply ground dark pepper

Directions:

1. Spread the diced strawberries over a medium serving platter or shallow serving bowl. In the event that the strawberries aren't sufficiently sweet exactly as you would prefer, hurl them with a touch of nectar or maple syrup.

2. Sprinkle the disintegrated goat cheddar over the strawberries, trailed by the hacked basil. Shower the olive oil and balsamic vinegar on top.

3. Polish off the plate of mixed greens with the salt, a couple of bits of crisply ground dark pepper, and the saved basil leaves. For the most excellent introduction, serve the plate of mixed greens speedily.

Scraps will keep well in the fridge, however, for around 3 days.

Turmeric Cauliflower And Cod Stew Servings: 4

Cooking Time: 30 Minutes

Ingredients:

½ pound cauliflower florets

1-pound cod fillets, boneless, skinless and cubed 1 tablespoons olive oil

1 yellow onion, chopped

½ teaspoon cumin seeds

1 green chili, chopped

¼ teaspoon turmeric powder

2 tomatoes chopped

A pinch of salt and black pepper

½ cup chicken stock

1 tablespoon cilantro, chopped

Directions:

1. Heat up a pot with the oil over medium heat, add the onion, chili, cumin and turmeric, stir and cook for 5 minutes.

2. Add the cauliflower, the fish and the other ingredients, toss, bring to a simmer and cook over medium heat for 25 minutes more.

3. Divide the stew into bowls and serve.

Nutrition Info: calories 281, fat 6, fiber 4, carbs 8, protein 12

Walnuts And Asparagus Delight Servings: 4

Cooking Time: 5 Minutes

Ingredients:

1 and ½ tablespoons olive oil

¾ pound asparagus, trimmed

¼ cup walnuts, chopped

Sunflower seeds and pepper to taste

Directions:

1. Place a skillet over medium heat add olive oil and let it heat up.

2. Add asparagus, Sauté for 5 minutes until browned.

3. Season with sunflower seeds and pepper.

4. Remove heat.

5. Add walnuts and toss.

Nutrition Info: Calories: 124Fat: 12gCarbohydrates: 2gProtein: 3g

Alfredo Zucchini Pasta Ingredients:

2 medium zucchinis spiralized

1-2 TB Vegan Parmesan (discretionary)

Fast Alfredo Sauce

1/2 cup crude cashews drenched for a couple of hours or in bubbling water for 10 minutes

2 TB lemon juice

3 TB nourishing yeast

2 tsp white miso (can sub tamari, soy sauce, or coconut aminos)

1 tsp onion powder

1/2 tsp garlic powder

1/4-1/2 cup water

Directions:

1. Spiralize zucchini noodles.

2. Add all alfredo fixings to a fast blender (beginning with 1/4 cup of water) and mix until smooth. In the event that your sauce is excessively thick,

include more water a tablespoon at once until you get the consistency you're searching for.

3. Top zucchini noodles with alfredo sauce and on the off chance that you'd like, some vegetarian pram.

Quinoa Turkey Chicken_Ingredients:

1 cup quinoa, flushed

3-1/2 cups water, isolated

1/2-pound lean ground turkey

1 enormous sweet onion, slashed

1 medium sweet red pepper, slashed

4 garlic cloves, minced

1 tablespoon bean stew powder

1 tablespoon ground cumin

1/2 teaspoon ground cinnamon

2 jars (15 ounces each) dark beans, flushed and depleted 1 can (28 ounces) squashed tomatoes

1 medium zucchini, slashed

1 chipotle pepper in adobo sauce, slashed

1 tablespoon adobo sauce

1 narrows leaf

1 teaspoon dried oregano

1/2 teaspoon salt

1/4 teaspoon pepper

1 cup solidified corn, defrosted

1/4 cup minced crisp cilantro

Discretionary garnishes: Cubed avocado, destroyed Monterey Jack cheddar

Directions:

1. In an enormous pan, heat quinoa and 2 cups water to the point of boiling. Decrease heat; spread and stew for 12-15 minutes or until water is retained. Expel from the warmth; lighten with a fork and put in a safe spot.

2. Then, in an enormous pan covered with cooking shower, cook the turkey, onion, red pepper and garlic over medium warmth until meat is never again pink and vegetables are delicate; channel. Mix in the bean stew powder, cumin and cinnamon; cook 2 minutes longer.

Whenever wanted, present with discretionary garnishes.

3. Include the dark beans, tomatoes, zucchini, chipotle pepper, adobo sauce, sound leaf, oregano, salt, pepper and remaining water.

Heat to the point of boiling. Diminish heat; spread and stew for 30

minutes. Mix in corn and quinoa; heat through. Dispose of narrows leaf; mix in cilantro. Present with discretionary fixings as wanted.

4. Freeze alternative: Freeze cooled stew in cooler compartments.

To utilize, incompletely defrost in fridge medium-term. Warmth through in a pot, blending once in a while; include juices or water if vital.

Garlic & Squash Noodles Servings: 4

Cooking Time: 15 Minutes

Ingredients:

For Preparing Sauce

¼ Cup coconut milk

6 Large dates

2/3g Gritted coconut

6 Garlic cloves

2tbsp Ginger paste

2tbsp Red curry paste

For Preparing Noodles

1 Large boil squash noodles

½ Julienne cut carrots

½ Julienne cut zucchini

1 small red bell pepper

¼ Cup cashew nuts

Directions:

1. For making sauce, blend all the ingredients and make a thick puree.

2. Cut spaghetti squash lengthwise and make noodles.

3. Lightly brush the baking tray with olive oil and bake squash noodles at 40C for 5-6 minutes.

4. For serving, incorporate noodles and puree in a bowl. Or serve puree alongside the noodles.

Nutrition Info: Calories 405 Carbs: 107g Fat: 28g Protein: 7g

Steamed Trout With Red Bean And Chili Salsa

Servings: 1

Cooking Time: 16 Minutes

Ingredients:

4 ½ oz cherry tomatoes, halved

1/4 avocado, unpeeled

6 oz skinless ocean trout fillet

Coriander leaves to serve

2 teaspoons olive oil

Lime wedges, to serve

4 ½ oz canned red kidney beans, rinsed and drained 1/2 red onion, thinly sliced

1 tablespoon pickled jalapenos, drained

1/2 teaspoon ground cumin

4 Sicilian olives/green olives

Directions:

1. Put a steamer basket over a pot of simmering water. Add fish to the basket and cover, cook for 10-12 minutes.

2. Remove the fish, then let it rest for a few minutes. In the meantime, preheat some oil in a pan.

3. Add pickled jalapenos, red kidney beans, olives, 1/2 teaspoon cumin, and cherry tomatoes. Cook for about 4-5 minutes, stirring continuously.

4. Scoop the bean batter onto a serving platter, followed by trout.

Add coriander and onion on top.

5. Serve along with lime wedges and avocado. Enjoy steamed ocean trout with red bean and chili salsa!

Nutrition Info: 243 calories 33.2 g fat 18.8 g total carbs 44 g protein

Sweet Potato And Turkey Soup *Servings: 4*

Cooking Time: 45 Minutes

Ingredients:

2 tablespoons olive oil

1 yellow onion, chopped

1 green bell pepper, chopped

2 sweet potatoes, peeled and cubed

1-pound turkey breast, skinless, boneless and cubed 1 teaspoon coriander, ground

A pinch of salt and black pepper

1 teaspoon sweet paprika

6 cups chicken stock

Juice of 1 lime

A handful parsley, chopped

Directions:

1. Heat up a pot with the oil over medium heat, add the onion, the bell pepper and the sweet potatoes, stir and cook for 5 minutes.

2. Add the meat and brown for 5 minutes more.

3. Add the rest of the ingredients, toss, bring to a simmer and cook over medium heat for 35 minutes more.

4. Ladle the soup into bowls and serve.

<u>Nutrition Info:</u> calories 203, fat 5, fiber 4, carbs 7, protein 8

Miso Broiled Salmon *Servings: 2*

Cooking Time: 20 Minutes

Ingredients:

2 tbsp. Maple Syrup

2 Lemons

¼ cup Miso

¼ tsp. Pepper, grounded

2 Limes

2 ½ lb. Salmon, skin-on

Dash of Cayenne Pepper

2 tbsp. Extra Virgin Olive Oil

¼ cup Miso

Directions:

1. First, mix the lime juice and lemon juice in a small bowl until combined well.

2. Next, spoon in the miso, cayenne pepper, maple syrup, olive oil, and pepper to it. Combine well.

3. Then, place the salmon on a parchment paper-lined baking sheet with the skin side down.

4. Brush the salmon generously with the miso lemon mixture.

5. Now, place the halved lemon and lime pieces on the sides with the cut side up.

6. Finally, bake them for 8 to 12 minutes or until the fish flakes.

Nutrition Info: Calories: 230KcalProteins: 28.3gCarbohydrates: 6.7gFat: 8.7g

Simply Sautéed Flaky Fillet *Servings: 6*

Cooking Time: 8 Minutes

Ingredients:

6-fillets tilapia

2-Tbsp.s olive oil

1-pc lemon, juice

Salt and pepper to taste

¼-cup parsley or cilantro, chopped

Directions:

1. Sauté tilapia fillets with olive oil in a medium-sized skillet placed over medium heat. Cook for 4 minutes on each side until the fish flakes easily with a fork.

2. Add salt and pepper to taste. Pour the lemon juice to each fillet.

3. To serve, sprinkle the cooked fillets with chopped parsley or cilantro.

Nutrition Info: Calories: 249 CalFat: 8.3 g Protein: 18.6 g Carbs: 25.9

Fiber: 1 g

Pork Carnitas <u>Servings: 10</u>

Cooking Time: 8 Hrs. 10 Minutes

Ingredients:

5 lbs. pork shoulder

2 garlic cloves, minced

1 tsp black pepper

1/4 tsp cinnamon

1 tsp dried oregano

1 tsp ground cumin

1 bay leaf

2 oz chicken broth

1 tsp lime juice

1 tbsp chili powder

1 tbsp salt

Directions:

1. Add pork along with the rest of the ingredients in a Slow Cooker.

2. Put on its lid and cook for 8 hrs. on low heat.

3. Once done, shred the cooked pork using a fork.

4. Spread this shredded pork on a baking tray.

5. Broil for 10 minutes then serve.

Nutrition Info: Calories 547 Fat 39 g, Carbs 2.6 g, Fiber 0 g, Protein 43 g

White Fish Chowder With Vegetables

Servings: 6 To 8

Cooking Time: 32 To 35 Minutes

Ingredients:

3 sweet potatoes, peeled and cut into ½-inch pieces 4 carrots, peeled and cut into ½-inch pieces 3 cups full-fat coconut milk

2 cups water

1 teaspoon dried thyme

½ teaspoon sea salt

10½ ounces (298 g) white fish, skinless and firm, such as cod or halibut, cut into chunks

Directions:

1. Add the sweet potatoes, carrots, coconut milk, water, thyme, and sea salt to a large saucepan over high heat, and bring to a boil.

2. Reduce the heat to low, cover, and simmer for 20 minutes until the vegetables are tender, stirring occasionally.

3. Pour half of the soup to a blender and purée until thoroughly mixed and smooth, then return it to the pot.

4. Stir in the fish chunks and continue cooking for an additional 12 to 15 minutes, or until the fish is cooked through.

5. Remove from the heat and serve in bowls.

Nutrition Info: calories: 450 ; fat: 28.7g ; protein: 14.2g ; carbs: 38.8g ; fiber: 8.1g ; sugar: 6.7g; sodium: 250mg

Lemony Mussels _Servings: 4_

Ingredients:

1 tbsp. extra virgin extra virgin olive oil 2 minced garlic cloves

2 lbs. scrubbed mussels

Juice of one lemon

Directions:

1. Put some water in a pot, add mussels, bring with a boil over medium heat, cook for 5 minutes, discard unopened mussels and transfer them with a bowl.

2. In another bowl, mix the oil with garlic and freshly squeezed lemon juice, whisk well, and add over the mussels, toss and serve.

3. Enjoy!

Nutrition Info: Calories: 140, Fat:4 g, Carbs:8 g, Protein:8 g, Sugars: 4g, Sodium:600 mg,

Lime & Chili Salmon Servings: 2

Cooking Time: 8 Minutes

Ingredients:

1 lb. salmon

1 tablespoon lime juice

½ teaspoon pepper

½ teaspoon chili powder

4 lime slices

Directions:

1. Drizzle salmon with lime juice.

2. Sprinkle both sides with pepper and chili powder.

3. Add salmon to the air fryer.

4. Place lime slices on top of salmon.

5. Air fry at 375 degrees F for 8 minutes.

Cheesy Tuna Pasta _Servings: 3-4_

Ingredients:

2 c. arugula

¼ c. chopped green onions

1 tbs. red vinegar

5 oz. drained canned tuna

¼ tsp. black pepper

2 oz. cooked whole-wheat pasta

1 tbsp. olive oil

1 tbsp. grated low-fat parmesan

Directions:

1. Cook the pasta in unsalted water until ready. Drain and set aside.

2. In a bowl of large size, thoroughly mix the tuna, green onions, vinegar, oil, arugula, pasta, and black pepper.

3. Toss well and top with the cheese.

4. Serve and enjoy.

<u>Nutrition Info:</u> Calories: 566.3, Fat:42.4 g, Carbs:18.6 g, Protein:29.8 g, Sugars:0.4 g, Sodium:688.6 mg

Coconut Crusted Fish Strips <u>*Servings: 4*</u>

Cooking Time: 12 Minutes

Ingredients:

Marinade

1 tablespoon soy sauce

1 teaspoon ground ginger

½ cup coconut milk

2 tablespoons maple syrup

½ cup pineapple juice

2 teaspoons hot sauce

Fish

1 lb. fish fillet, sliced into strips

Pepper to taste

1 cup breadcrumbs

1 cup coconut flakes (unsweetened)

Cooking spray

Directions:

1. Mix marinade ingredients in a bowl.

2. Stir in fish strips.

3. Cover and refrigerate for 2 hours.

4. Preheat your air fryer to 375 degrees F.

5. In a bowl, mix pepper, breadcrumbs and coconut flakes.

6. Dip fish strips in the breadcrumb mixture.

7. Spray your air fryer basket with oil.

8. Add fish strips to the air fryer basket.

9. Air fry for 6 minutes per side.

Mexican Fish *Servings: 2*

Cooking Time: 10 Minutes

Ingredients:

4 fish fillets

2 teaspoons Mexican oregano

4 teaspoons cumin

4 teaspoons chili powder

Pepper to taste

Cooking spray

Directions:

1. Preheat your air fryer to 400 degrees F.

2. Spray fish with oil.

3. Season both sides of fish with spices and pepper.

4. Place fish in the air fryer basket.

5. Cook for 5 minutes.

6. Flip and cook for another 5 minutes.

Trout With Cucumber Salsa Servings: 4

Cooking Time: 10 Minutes

Ingredients:

Salsa:

1 English cucumber, diced

¼ cup unsweetened coconut yogurt

2 tablespoons chopped fresh mint

1 scallion, white and green parts, chopped

1 teaspoon raw honey

Sea salt

Fish:

4 (5-ounce) trout fillets, patted dry

1 tablespoon olive oil

Sea salt and freshly ground black pepper, to taste Directions:

1. Make the salsa: Stir together the yogurt, cucumber, mint, scallion, honey, and sea salt in a small bowl until completely mixed. Set aside.

2. On a clean work surface, rub the trout fillets lightly with sea salt and pepper.

3. Heat the olive oil in a large skillet over medium heat. Add the trout fillets to the hot skillet and panfry for about 10 minutes, flipping the fish halfway through, or until the fish is cooked to your liking.

4. Spread the salsa on top of the fish and serve.

Nutrition Info: calories: 328 ; fat: 16.2g ; protein: 38.9g ; carbs: 6.1g

; fiber: 1.0g ; sugar: 3.2g; sodium: 477mg

Lemon Zoodles With Shrimp *Servings: 4*

Cooking Time: 0 Minutes

Ingredients:

Sauce:

½ cup packed fresh basil leaves

Juice of 1 lemon (or 3 tablespoons)

1 teaspoon bottled minced garlic

Pinch sea salt

Pinch freshly ground black pepper

¼ cup canned full-fat coconut milk

1 large yellow squash, julienned or spiralized 1 large zucchini, julienned or spiralized

1 pound (454 g) shrimp, deveined, boiled, peeled, and chilled Zest of 1 lemon (optional)

Directions:

1. Make the sauce: Process the basil leaves, lemon juice, garlic, sea salt, and pepper in a food processor until chopped thoroughly.

2. Slowly pour in the coconut milk while the processor is still running. Pulse until smooth.

3. Transfer the sauce to a large bowl, along with the yellow squash and zucchini. Toss well.

4. Scatter the shrimp and lemon zest (if desired) on top of the noodles. Serve immediately.

Nutrition Info: calories: 246 ; fat: 13.1g ; protein: 28.2g ; carbs: 4.9g

; fiber: 2.0g ; sugar: 2.8g; sodium: 139mg

Crispy Shrimp *Servings: 4*

Cooking Time: 3 Minutes

Ingredients:

1 lb. shrimp, peeled and deveined

½ cup fish breading mix

Cooking spray

Directions:

1. Preheat your air fryer to 390 degrees F.

2. Spray shrimp with oil.

3. Coat with the breading mix.

4. Spray air fryer basket with oil.

5. Add shrimp to air fryer basket.

6. Cook for 3 minutes.

Broiled Sea Bass Servings: 2

Ingredients:

2 minced garlic cloves

Pepper.

1 tbsp. lemon juice

2 white sea bass fillets

¼ tsp. herb seasoning blend

Directions:

1. Spray a broiler pan with some olive oil and place the fillets on it.

2. Sprinkle the lemon juice, garlic and the spices over the fillets.

3. Broil for about 10 min or until the fish is golden.

4. Serve over a bed of sautéed spinach if desired.

Nutrition Info: Calories: 169, Fat:9.3 g, Carbs:0.34 g, Protein:15.3 g, Sugars:0.2 g, Sodium:323 mg

Salmon Cakes *Servings: 4*

Cooking Time: 10 Minutes

Ingredients:

Cooking spray

1 lb. salmon fillet, flaked

¼ cup almond flour

2 teaspoons Old Bay seasoning

1 green onion, chopped

Directions:

1. Preheat your air fryer to 390 degrees F.

2. Spray your air fryer basket with oil.

3. In a bowl, combine the remaining ingredients.

4. Form patties from the mixture.

5. Spray both sides of patties with oil.

6. Air fry for 8 minutes.

Spicy Cod _Servings: 4_

Ingredients:

2 tbsps. Fresh chopped parsley

2 lbs. cod fillets

2 c. low sodium salsa

1 tbsp. flavorless oil

Directions:

1. Preheat the oven to 350°F.

2. In a large, deep baking dish drizzle the oil along the bottom.

Place the cod fillets in the dish. Pour the salsa over the fish. Cover with foil for 20 minutes. Remove the foil last 10 minutes of cooking.

3. Bake in the oven for 20 – 30 minutes, until the fish is flaky.

4. Serve with white or brown rice. Garnish with parsley.

Nutrition Info: Calories: 110, Fat:11 g, Carbs:83 g, Protein:16.5 g, Sugars:0 g, Sodium:122 mg

Smoked Trout Spread Servings: 2

Ingredients:

2 tsps. Fresh lemon juice

½ c. low-fat cottage cheese

1 diced celery stalk

¼ lb. skinned smoked trout fillet,

½ tsp. Worcestershire sauce

1 tsp. hot pepper sauce

¼ c. coarsely chopped red onion

Directions:

1. Combine the trout, cottage cheese, red onion, lemon juice, hot pepper sauce and Worcestershire sauce in a blender or food processor.

2. Process until smooth, stopping to scrape down the sides of the bowl as needed.

3. Fold in the diced celery.

4. Keep in an air-tight container in the refrigerator.

Nutrition Info: Calories: 57, Fat:4 g, Carbs:1 g, Protein:4 g, Sugars:0 g, Sodium:660 mg

Tuna And Shallots Servings: 4

Ingredients:

½ c. low-sodium chicken stock

1 tbsp. olive oil

4 boneless and skinless tuna fillets

2 chopped shallots

1 tsp. sweet paprika

2 tbsps. lime juice

¼ tsp. black pepper

Directions:

1. Heat up a pan with the oil over medium-high heat, add shallots and sauté for 3 minutes.

2. Add the fish and cook it for 4 minutes on each side.

3. Add the rest of the ingredients, cook everything for 3 minutes more, divide between plates and serve.

Nutrition Info: Calories: 4040, Fat:34.6 g, Carbs:3 g, Protein:21.4 g, Sugars:0.5 g, Sodium:1000 mg

Lemon Pepper Shrimp *Servings: 2*

Cooking Time: 10 Minutes

Ingredients:

1 tablespoon lemon juice

1 tablespoon olive oil

1 teaspoon lemon pepper

¼ teaspoon garlic powder

¼ teaspoon paprika

12 oz. shrimp, peeled and deveined

Directions:

1. Preheat your air fryer to 400 degrees F.

2. Mix lemon juice, olive oil, lemon pepper, garlic powder and paprika in a bowl.

3. Stir in shrimp and coat evenly with the mixture.

4. Add to the air fryer.

5. Cook for 8 minutes.

Hot Tuna Steak *Servings: 6*

Ingredients:

2 tbsps. Fresh lemon juice

Pepper.

Roasted orange garlic mayonnaise

¼ c. whole black peppercorns

6 sliced tuna steaks

2 tbsps. Extra-virgin olive oil

Salt

Directions:

1. Place the tuna in a bowl to fit. Add the oil, lemon juice, salt and pepper. Turn the tuna to coat well in the marinade. Let rest 15 to 20

minutes, turning once.

2. Place the peppercorns in a double thickness of plastic bags. Tap the peppercorns with a heavy saucepan or small mallet to crush them coarsely. Place on a large plate.

3. When ready to cook the tuna, dip the edges into the crushed peppercorns. Heat a nonstick skillet over medium heat. Sear the tuna steaks, in batches if necessary, for 4 minutes per side for medium-rare fish, adding 2 to 3 tablespoons of the marinade to the skillet if necessary, to prevent sticking.

4. Serve dolloped with roasted orange garlic mayonnaise Nutrition Info: Calories: 124, Fat:0.4 g, Carbs:0.6 g, Protein:28 g, Sugars:0 g, Sodium:77 mg

Cajun Salmon _Servings: 2_

Cooking Time: 10 Minutes

Ingredients:

2 salmon fillets

Cooking spray

1 tablespoon Cajun seasoning

1 tablespoon honey

Directions:

1. Preheat your air fryer to 390 degrees F.

2. Spray both sides of fish with oil.

3. Sprinkle with Cajun seasoning.

4. Spray air fryer basket with oil.

5. Add salmon to the air fryer basket.

6. Air fry for 10 minutes.

Quinoa Salmon Bowl With Vegetables

Servings: 4

Cooking Time: 0 Minutes

Ingredients:

1 pound (454 g) cooked salmon, flaked

4 cups cooked quinoa

6 radishes, thinly sliced

1 zucchini, sliced into half moons

3 cups arugula

3 scallions, minced

½ cup almond oil

1 teaspoon sugar-free hot sauce

1 tablespoon apple cider vinegar

1 teaspoon sea salt

½ cup toasted slivered almonds, for garnish (optional) Directions:

1. In a large bowl, mix together the flaked salmon, cooked quinoa, radishes, zucchini, arugula, and scallions, and stir well.

2. Fold in the almond oil, hot sauce, apple cider vinegar, and sea salt and toss to combine.

3. Divide the mixture into four bowls. Scatter each bowl evenly with the slivered almonds for garnish, if desired. Serve immediately.

Nutrition Info: calories: 769 ; fat: 51.6g ; protein: 37.2g ; carbs: 44.8g ; fiber: 8.0g ; sugar: 4.0g; sodium: 681mg

Crumbed Fish *Servings: 4*

Cooking Time: 15 Minutes

Ingredients:

¼ cup olive oil

1 cup dry breadcrumbs

4 white fish fillets

Pepper to taste

Directions:

1. Preheat your air fryer to 350 degrees F.

2. Sprinkle both sides of fish with pepper.

3. Combine oil and breadcrumbs in a bowl.

4. Dip the fish into the mixture.

5. Press breadcrumbs to adhere.

6. Place fish in the air fryer.

7. Cook for 15 minutes.

Simple Salmon Patties *Servings: 4*

Cooking Time: 8 To 10 Minutes

Ingredients:

1 pound (454 g) skinless boned salmon fillets, minced ¼ cup minced sweet onion

½ cup almond flour

2 garlic cloves, minced

2 eggs, whisked

1 teaspoon Dijon mustard

1 tablespoon freshly squeezed lemon juice

Dash red pepper flakes

½ teaspoon sea salt

¼ teaspoon freshly ground black pepper

1 tablespoon avocado oil

Directions:

1. Mix together the minced salmon, sweet onion, almond flour, garlic, whisked eggs, mustard, lemon juice, red pepper flakes, sea salt, and pepper in a large bowl, and stir until well incorporated.

2. Allow the salmon mixture to rest for 5 minutes.

3. Scoop out the salmon mixture and shape into four ½-inch-thick patties with your hands.

4. Heat the avocado oil in a large skillet over medium heat. Add the patties to the hot skillet and cook each side for 4 to 5 minutes until lightly browned and cooked through.

5. Remove from the heat and serve on a plate.

Nutrition Info: calories: 248 ; fat: 13.4g ; protein: 28.4g ; carbs: 4.1g ; fiber: 2.0g ; sugar: 2.0g; sodium: 443mg

Popcorn Shrimp *Servings: 4*

Cooking Time: 10 Minutes

Ingredients:

½ teaspoon onion powder

½ teaspoon garlic powder

½ teaspoon paprika

¼ teaspoon ground mustard

⅛ teaspoon dried sage

⅛ teaspoon ground thyme

⅛ teaspoon dried oregano

⅛ teaspoon dried basil

Pepper to taste

3 tablespoons cornstarch

1 lb. shrimp, peeled and deveined

Cooking spray

Directions:

1. Combine all ingredients except shrimp in a bowl.

2. Coat shrimp with the mixture.

3. Spray air fryer basket with oil.

4. Preheat your air fryer to 390 degrees F.

5. Add shrimp inside.

6. Air fry for 4 minutes.

7. Shake the basket.

8. Cook for another 5 minutes.

Spicy Baked Fish Servings: 5

Ingredients:

1 tbsp. olive oil

1 tsp. spice salt free seasoning

1 lb. salmon fillet

Directions:

1. Preheat the oven to 350F.

2. Sprinkle the fish with olive oil and the seasoning.

3. Bake for 15 min uncovered.

4. Slice and serve.

Nutrition Info: Calories: 192, Fat:11 g, Carbs:14.9 g, Protein:33.1 g, Sugars:0.3 g, Sodium:505 6 mg

Paprika Tuna Servings: 4

Ingredients:

½ tsp. chili powder

2 tsps. sweet paprika

¼ tsp. black pepper

2 tbsps. olive oil

4 boneless tuna steaks

Directions:

1. Heat up a pan with the oil over medium-high heat, add the tuna steaks, season with paprika, black pepper and chili powder, cook for 5 minutes on each side, divide between plates and serve with a side salad.

Nutrition Info: Calories: 455, Fat:20.6 g, Carbs:0.8 g, Protein:63.8

g, Sugars:7.4 g, Sodium: 411 mg

Fish Patties Servings: 2

Cooking Time: 7 Minutes

Ingredients:

8 oz. white fish fillet, flaked

Garlic powder to taste

1 teaspoon lemon juice

Directions:

1. Preheat your air fryer to 390 degrees F.

2. Combine all the ingredients.

3. Form patties from the mixture.

4. Place fish patties in the air fryer.

5. Cook for 7 minutes.

Seared Scallops With Honey *Servings: 4*

Cooking Time: 15 Minutes

Ingredients:

1 pound (454 g) large scallops, rinsed and patted dry Dash sea salt

Dash freshly ground black pepper

2 tablespoons avocado oil

¼ cup raw honey

3 tablespoons coconut aminos

1 tablespoon apple cider vinegar

2 garlic cloves, minced

Directions:

1. In a bowl, add the scallops, sea salt, and pepper and toss until coated well.

2. In a large skillet, heat the avocado oil over medium-high heat.

3. Sear the scallops for 2 to 3 minutes on each side, or until the scallops turn milky white or opaque and firm.

4. Remove the scallops from the heat to a plate and loosely tent with foil to keep warm. Set aside.

5. Add the honey, coconut aminos, vinegar, and garlic to the skillet and stir well.

6. Bring to a simmer and cook for about 7 minutes until the liquid is reduced, stirring occasionally.

7. Return the seared scallops to the skillet, stirring to coat them with the glaze.

8. Divide the scallops among four plates and serve warm.

Nutrition Info: calories: 382 ; fat: 18.9g ; protein: 21.2g ; carbs: 26.1g ; fiber: 1.0g ; sugar: 17.7g; sodium: 496mg

Cod Fillets With Shiitake Mushrooms *Servings: 4*

Cooking Time: 15 To 18 Minutes

Ingredients:

1 garlic clove, minced

1 leek, thinly sliced

1 teaspoon minced fresh ginger root

1 tablespoon olive oil

½ cup dry white wine

½ cup sliced shiitake mushrooms

4 (6-ounce / 170-g) cod fillets

1 teaspoon sea salt

⅛ teaspoon freshly ground black pepper

Directions:

1. Preheat the oven to 375ºF (190ºC).

2. Mix together the garlic, leek, ginger root, wine, olive oil, and mushrooms in a baking pan, and toss until the mushrooms are evenly coated.

3. Bake in the preheated oven for 10 minutes until lightly browned.

4. Remove the baking pan from the oven. Spread the cod fillets on top and season with sea salt and pepper.

5. Cover with aluminum foil and return to the oven. Bake for 5 to 8 minutes more, or until the fish is flaky.

6. Remove the aluminum foil and cool for 5 minutes before serving.

Nutrition Info: calories: 166 ; fat: 6.9g ; protein: 21.2g ; carbs: 4.8g ; fiber: 1.0g ; sugar: 1.0g; sodium: 857mg

Broiled White Sea Bass Servings: 2

Ingredients:

1 tsp. minced garlic

Ground black pepper

1 tbsp. lemon juice

8 oz. white sea bass fillets

¼ tsp. salt-free herbed seasoning blend

Directions:

1. Preheat the broiler and position the rack 4 inches from the heat source.

2. Lightly spray a baking pan with cooking spray. Place the fillets in the pan. Sprinkle the lemon juice, garlic, herbed seasoning and pepper over the fillets.

3. Broil until the fish is opaque throughout when tested with a tip of a knife, about 8 to 10 minutes.

4. Serve immediately.

Nutrition Info: Calories: 114, Fat:2 g, Carbs:2 g, Protein:21 g, Sugars:0.5 g, Sodium:78 mg

Baked Tomato Hake *Servings: 4-5*

Ingredients:

½ c. tomato sauce

1 tbsp. olive oil

Parsley

2 sliced tomatoes

½ c. grated cheese

4 lbs. de-boned and sliced hake fish

Salt.

Directions:

1. Preheat the oven to 400 0F.

2. Season the fish with salt.

3. In a skillet or saucepan; stir-fry the fish in the olive oil until half-done.

4. Take four foil papers to cover the fish.

5. Shape the foil to resemble containers; add the tomato sauce into each foil container.

6. Add the fish, tomato slices, and top with grated cheese.

7. Bake until you get a golden crust, for approximately 20-25 minutes.

8. Open the packs and top with parsley.

Nutrition Info: Calories: 265, Fat:15 g, Carbs:18 g, Protein:22 g, Sugars:0.5 g, Sodium:94.6 mg

Seared Haddock With Beets _Servings: 4_

Cooking Time: 30 Minutes

Ingredients:

8 beets, peeled and cut into eighths

2 shallots, thinly sliced

2 tablespoons apple cider vinegar

2 tablespoons olive oil, divided

1 teaspoon bottled minced garlic

1 teaspoon chopped fresh thyme

Pinch sea salt

4 (5-ounce / 142-g) haddock fillets, patted dry Directions:

1. Preheat the oven to 400ºF (205ºC).

2. Combine the beets, shallots, vinegar, 1 tablespoon of olive oil, garlic, thyme, and sea salt in a medium bowl, and toss to coat well.

Spread out the beet mixture in a baking dish.

3. Roast in the preheated oven for about 30 minutes, turning once or twice with a spatula, or until the beets are tender.

4. Meanwhile, heat the remaining 1 tablespoon of olive oil in a large skillet over medium-high heat.

5. Add the haddock and sear each side for 4 to 5 minutes, or until the flesh is opaque and it flakes apart easily.

6. Transfer the fish to a plate and serve topped with the roasted beets.

Nutrition Info: calories: 343 ; fat: 8.8g ; protein: 38.1g ; carbs: 20.9g

; fiber: 4.0g ; sugar: 11.5g; sodium: 540mg

Heartfelt Tuna Melt _Servings: 4_

Ingredients:

3 oz. grated reduced-fat cheddar cheese

1/3 c. chopped celery

Black pepper and salt

¼ c. chopped onion

2 whole-wheat English muffins

6 oz. drained white tuna

¼ c. low fat Russian

Directions:

1. Preheat broiler. Combine tuna, celery, onion and salad dressing.

2. Season with salt and pepper.

3. Toast English muffin halves.

4. Place split-side-up on baking sheet and top each with 1/4 of tuna mixture.

5. Broil 2-3 minutes or until heated through.

6. Top with cheese and return to broiler until cheese is melted, about 1 minute longer.

Nutrition Info: Calories: 320, Fat:16.7 g, Carbs:17.1 g, Protein:25.7 g, Sugars:5.85 g, Sodium:832 mg

Lemon Salmon With Kaffir Lime Servings: 8

Ingredients:

1 quartered and bruised lemon grass stalk

2 kaffir torn lime leaves

1 thinly sliced lemon

1 ½ c. fresh coriander leaves

1 whole side salmon fillet

Directions:

1. Pre-heat the oven to 350°F.

2. Cover a baking pan with foil sheets, overlapping the sides 3. Place the Salmon on the foil, top with the lemon, lime leaves, the lemon grass and 1 cup of the coriander leaves. Option: season with salt and pepper.

4. Bring the long side of the foil to the center before folding the seal.

Roll the ends in order to close up the salmon.

5. Bake for 30 minutes.

6. Transfer the cooked fish to a platter. Top with fresh coriander.

Serve with white or brown rice.

Nutrition Info: Calories: 103, Fat:11.8 g, Carbs:43.5 g, Protein:18 g, Sugars:0.7 g, Sodium:322 mg

Tender Salmon In Mustard Sauce Servings: 2

Ingredients:

5 tbsps. Minced dill

2/3 c. sour cream

Pepper.

2 tbsps. Dijon mustard

1 tsp. garlic powder

5 oz. salmon fillets

2-3 tbsps. Lemon juice

Directions:

1. Mix sour cream, mustard, lemon juice and dill.

2. Season the fillets with pepper and garlic powder.

3. Arrange the salmon on a baking sheet skin side down and cover with the prepared mustard sauce.

4. Bake for 20 minutes at 390°F.

<u>Nutrition Info:</u> Calories: 318, Fat:12 g, Carbs:8 g, Protein:40.9 g, Sugars:909.4 g, Sodium:1.4 mg

Crab Salad Servings: 4

Ingredients:

2 c. crab meat

1 c. halved cherry tomatoes

1 tbsp. olive oil

Black pepper

1 chopped shallot

1/3 c. chopped cilantro

1 tbsp. lemon juice

Directions:

1. In a bowl, combine the crab with the tomatoes and the other ingredients, toss and serve.

Nutrition Info: Calories: 54, Fat:3.9 g, Carbs:2.6 g, Protein:2.3 g, Sugars:2.3 g, Sodium:462.5 mg

Baked Salmon With Miso Sauce Servings: 4

Cooking Time: 15 To 20 Minutes

Ingredients:

Sauce:

¼ cup apple cider

¼ cup white miso

1 tablespoon olive oil

1 tablespoon white rice vinegar

⅛ teaspoon ground ginger

4 (3- to 4-ounce / 85- to 113-g) boneless salmon fillets 1 sliced scallion, for garnish

⅛ teaspoon red pepper flakes, for garnish

Directions:

1. Preheat the oven to 375ºF (190ºC).

2. Make the sauce: Whisk together the apple cider, white miso, olive oil, rice vinegar, ginger in a small bowl. Add a little water if a thinner consistency is desired.

3. Arrange the salmon fillets in a baking pan, skin-side down. Spoon the prepared sauce over the fillets to coat evenly.

4. Bake in the preheated oven for 15 to 20 minutes, or until the fish flakes easily with a fork.

5. Garnish with the sliced scallion and red pepper flakes and serve.

Nutrition Info: calories: 466 ; fat: 18.4g ; protein: 67.5g ; carbs: 9.1g

; fiber: 1.0g ; sugar: 2.7g; sodium: 819mg

Herb-coated Baked Cod With Honey _Servings: 2_

Ingredients:

6 tbsps. Herb-flavored stuffing

8 oz. cod fillets

2 tbsps. Honey

Directions:

1. Preheat your oven to 375 0F.

2. Spray a baking pan lightly with cooking spray.

3. Put the herb-flavored stuffing in a bag and close. Squash the stuffing until it gets crumbly.

4. Coat the fishes with honey and get rid of the remaining honey.

Add one fillet to the bag of stuffing and shake gently to coat the fish completely.

5. Transfer the cod to the baking pan and repeat the process for the second fish.

6. Wrap the fillets with foil and bake until firm and opaque all through when you test with the tip of a knife blade, about ten minutes.

7. Serve hot.

<u>Nutrition Info:</u> Calories: 185, Fat:1 g, Carbs:23 g, Protein:21 g, Sugars:2 g, Sodium:144.3 mg

Parmesan Cod Mix Servings: 4

Ingredients:

1 tbsp. lemon juice

½ c. chopped green onion

4 boneless cod fillets

3 minced garlic cloves

1 tbsp. olive oil

½ c. shredded low-fat parmesan cheese

Directions:

1. Heat up a pan with the oil over medium heat, add the garlic and the green onions, toss and sauté for 5 minutes.

2. Add the fish and cook it for 4 minutes on each side.

3. Add the lemon juice, sprinkle the parmesan on top, cook everything for 2 minutes more, divide between plates and serve.

Nutrition Info: Calories: 275, Fat:22.1 g, Carbs:18.2 g, Protein:12 g, Sugars:0.34 g, Sodium:285.4 mg

Crispy Garlic Shrimp _Servings: 4_

Cooking Time: 10 Minutes

Ingredients:

1 lb. shrimp, peeled and deveined

2 teaspoons garlic powder

Pepper to taste

¼ cup flour

Cooking spray

Directions:

1. Season shrimp with garlic powder and pepper.

2. Coat with flour.

3. Spray your air fryer basket with oil.

4. Add shrimp to the air fryer basket.

5. Cook at 400 degrees F for 10 minutes, shaking once halfway through.

Creamy Sea Bass Mix Servings: 4

Ingredients:

1 tbsp. chopped parsley

2 tbsps. avocado oil

1 c. coconut cream

1 tbsp. lime juice

1 chopped yellow onion

¼ tsp. black pepper

4 boneless sea bass fillets

Directions:

1. Heat up a pan with the oil over medium heat, add the onion, toss and sauté for 2 minutes.

2. Add the fish and cook it for 4 minutes on each side.

3. Add the rest of the ingredients, cook everything for 4 minutes more, divide between plates and serve.

Nutrition Info: Calories: 283, Fat:12.3 g, Carbs:12.5 g, Protein:8 g, Sugars:6 g, Sodium:508.8 mg

Cucumber Ahi Poke _Servings: 4_

Cooking Time: 0 Minutes

Ingredients:

Ahi Poke:

1 pound (454 g) sushi-grade ahi tuna, cut into 1-inch cubes 3 tablespoons coconut aminos

3 scallions, thinly sliced

1 serrano chile, deseeded and minced (optional) 1 teaspoon olive oil

1 teaspoon rice vinegar

1 teaspoon toasted sesame seeds

Dash ground ginger

1 large avocado, diced

1 cucumber, sliced into ½-inch-thick rounds Directions:

1. Make the ahi poke: Toss the ahi tuna cubes with the coconut aminos, scallions, serrano chile (if desired), olive oil, vinegar, sesame seeds, and ginger in a large bowl.

2. Cover the bowl with plastic wrap and marinate in the fridge for 15

minutes.

3. Add the diced avocado to the bowl of ahi poke and stir to incorporate.

4. Arrange the cucumber rounds on a serving plate. Spoon the ahi poke over the cucumber and serve.

Nutrition Info: calories: 213 ; fat: 15.1g ; protein: 10.1g ; carbs: 10.8g ; fiber: 4.0g ; sugar: 0.6g; sodium: 70mg

Minty Cod Mix *Servings: 4*

Ingredients:

4 boneless cod fillets

½ c. low-sodium chicken stock

2 tbsps. olive oil

¼ tsp. black pepper

1 tbsp. chopped mint

1 tsps. grated lemon zest

¼ c. chopped shallot

1 tbsp. lemon juice

Directions:

1. Heat up a pan with the oil over medium heat, add the shallots, stir and sauté for 5 minutes.

2. Add the cod, the lemon juice and the other ingredients, bring to a simmer and cook over medium heat for 12 minutes.

3. Divide everything between plates and serve.

Nutrition Info: Calories: 160, Fat:8.1 g, Carbs:2 g, Protein:20.5 g, Sugars:8 g, Sodium:45 mg

Lemony & Creamy Tilapia Servings: 4

Ingredients:

2 tbsps. Chopped fresh cilantro

¼ c. low-fat mayonnaise

Freshly ground black pepper

¼ c. fresh lemon juice

4 tilapia fillets

½ c. grated low-fat parmesan cheese

½ tsp. garlic powder

Directions:

1. In a bowl, mix together all ingredients except tilapia fillets and cilantro.

2. Coat the fillets with mayonnaise mixture evenly.

3. Place the filets onto a large foil paper. Wrap the foil paper around fillets to seal them.

4. Arrange the foil packet in the bottom of a large slow cooker.

5. Set the slow cooker on low.

6. Cover and cook for 3-4 hours.

7. Serve with the garnishing of cilantro.

Nutrition Info: Calories: 133.6, Fat:2.4 g, Carbs:4.6 g, Protein:22 g, Sugars:0.9 g, Sodium:510.4 mg

Fish Tacos Servings: 4

Cooking Time: 20 Minutes

Ingredients:

Cooking spray

1 tablespoon olive oil

4 cups cabbage slaw

1 tablespoon apple cider vinegar

1 tablespoon lime juice

Pinch cayenne pepper

Pepper to taste

2 tablespoons taco seasoning mix

¼ cup all-purpose flour

1 lb. cod fillet, sliced into cubes

4 corn tortillas

Directions:

1. Preheat your air fryer to 400 degrees F.

2. Spray your air fryer basket with oil.

3. In a bowl, mix the olive oil, cabbage slaw, vinegar, lime juice, cayenne pepper and pepper.

4. In another bowl, mix the taco seasoning and flour.

5. Coat the fish cubes with the taco seasoning mixture.

6. Add these to the air fryer basket.

7. Air fry for 10 minutes, shaking halfway through.

8. Top the corn tortillas with the fish and cabbage slaw mixture and roll them up.

Ginger Sea Bass Mix Servings: 4

Ingredients:

4 boneless sea bass fillets

2 tbsps. olive oil

1 tsp. grated ginger

1 tbsp. chopped cilantro

Black pepper

1 tbsp. balsamic vinegar

Directions:

1. Heat up a pan with the oil over medium heat, add the fish and cook for 5 minutes on each side.

2. Add the rest of the ingredients, cook everything for 5 minutes more, divide everything between plates and serve.

Nutrition Info: Calories: 267, Fat:11.2 g, Carbs:1.5 g, Protein:23 g, Sugars:0.78 g, Sodium:321.2 mg

www.ingramcontent.com/pod-product-compliance
Lightning Source LLC
Chambersburg PA
CBHW071819080526
44589CB00012B/853